CW00949682

When ideology enters the equation

Multiple forces are at work to silence scientists, writes **SALLY GIMSON**

SCIENCE, ACCORDING TO the Encyclopedia Britannica, is any system of knowledge concerned with the physical world and its phenomena, and which entails unbiased observations and systematic experimentation.

It should be so simple. Yet it's not because pursuing knowledge throws up inconvenient truths which trouble some rulers and populations. Ever since Galileo faced the Roman inquisition in the 17th century for arguing that the Earth went around the sun, scientists have risked being ruthlessly silenced.

In this issue, we show how ideology often stands in the way of scientific progress. Dissident author Murong

Xuecun explores how Chinese scientists are isolated from the wider scientific community and live in constant fear of arrest and worse. Ideology trumps scientific truth in a society that values obedience to the state over curiosity. Yet Murong concludes: "If Xi continues to rule in this way, it won't be long before China becomes a poor and backward country again."

India finds itself in similar danger, as our South Asia contributing editor Salil Tripathi reports. Prime Minister Narendra Modi has proved he is at least as keen on mythology as he is on scientific advancement. For instance, the Indian Institute of Technology in Mandi insists first-year engineering students study re-incarnation and out-of-body experiences.

But it is not just autocrats who cause a problem for science. In Europe, Cern, the European Organization for Nuclear Research, no longer allows the participation of researchers based in Russia or Belarus because of the Ukraine conflict. Preventing cooperation over nuclear research rarely ends well.

In the USA academics at Columbia University were so worried about Donald Trump's attitude to science, particularly to climate change research and abortion, that they set up the Silencing Science Tracker. Since the tracker was launched in 2018 some 531 cases of censorship, information suppression and misrepresentation of

scientific facts have been noted. Even under Joe Biden, the government has been slow to undo the damage.

In another exclusive investigation for Index, assistant editor Katie Dancey-Downs has looked at the use of animals in lab experiments. She has discovered that scientists who question the effectiveness of animal testing are told to shut up if they value their careers. This censorship is shocking, particularly as new and better techniques for testing new drugs, which don't involve animals, have now been developed.

Excitingly, we are proud to publish in English for the first time a story by banned Russian author Grigory Chkhartishvili aka Boris Akunin who won the Freedom to Publish Award (supported by Index) at the British Book Awards. We also interview Irish folk singer Christy Moore, whose song about the burning down of the Stardust nightclub in 1981 was banned.

Look out for chief executive Jemimah Steinfeld's reflections on whether change comes better from within, after David Neuberger KC controversially decided to remain a judge on Hong Kong's Court of Final Appeal. Also check out our article on political prisoners in Belarus, part of Index's project (and exhibition), Letters from Lukashenka's Prisoners. ✖

Sally Gimson is acting editor at Index

53(03):1/1|DOI:10.1177/03064220241285653

Cutting comments

Our cover artist turns propaganda on its head

BADIUCAO, THE COVER artist for this issue of Index on Censorship, calls himself a "Chinese Aussie artist hunted by the Chinese Government". Born in Shanghai, Badiucao had

no formal art training in China but comes from a long line of creatives — his grandfather and great uncle were filmmakers in China who paid for their work with their lives in the 1950s. Badiucao's art

is typified by the clever reworking of Communist propaganda imagery, subverting it to criticise the Chinese Communist Party. His cover revisits Andy Warhol's famous picture of Albert Einstein.

Elsewhere in this issue, Badiucao illustrates Murong Xuecun's article on Chinese science. Winter in Beijing shows a lonely dictator sitting on a broken dragon throne in heavy snow.

CONTENTS

Special Report: Inconvenient Truths

Corrections and clarifications

The following corrections relate to Index Vol.53 No.2

P.86 In poet Bänoo Zan's article, the second sentence should read "In dictatorships and totalitarian regimes, there is state censorship in the name of national security or cultural and religious identity." Zan has also published one book in Iran and two in Canada. The anthology that Zan is co-editing will be published in 2025 P.108 Kerala is a state in India P.110 Upender Gundala is an assistant professor in the Department of English at The English and Foreign Languages University (EFLU)

Comment

Culture

INDEXONCENSORSHIP.ORG

CREDIT: Badiucao

The Index

53(03):4/10|DOI:10.1177/03064220241285654

A round-up of
events in the
world of free
expression
from Index's
unparalleled
network of
writers and
activists.

Edited by
MARK STIMPSON

PICTURED: Vice President Kamala Harris greets Wall Street Journal reporter Evan Gershkovich after his release in a prisoner swap with Russia

The Index

LEFT TO RIGHT: Donald Trump - US; Salva Kiir Mayardit - South Sudan; Umaro Embalo - Guinea-Bissau

ELECTION WATCH

The bumper election year continues. Here's who is heading to the polls next

1. US presidential election

5 NOVEMBER 2024

In November, the US electorate will head to the polls to elect either Kamala Harris or Donald Trump as the country's new leader. Free expression issues in the US election have been well documented, with perhaps the most pressing concern being the level of disinformation spread during the campaign period, particularly online. Social media platform X has been the main offender, with questions being raised over the validity of the role played by its billionaire owner Elon Musk. Musk publicly endorsed Trump and has been accused of manipulating the platform's content. On one occasion he shared an AI-made video of Harris without clarifying that it was fake, which was a violation of the platform's own terms and conditions. Concerns were heightened when Trump declared that the US electorate "won't have to vote any more" if he was elected, sparking debate over his commitment to the democratic process. Further obstacles to free speech include electoral practices such as gerrymandering and implementing stricter voter ID laws which have been accused of being racially discriminatory.

2. South Sudan general election

22 DECEMBER 2024

The last general election held in South Sudan before it gained independence took place in 2010. An election scheduled for 2015 was repeatedly postponed after an alleged coup d'état in 2013 and an ensuing civil war.

A general election is now finally expected to take place on 22 December 2024 yet concerns have been raised that the country is not ready for elections. One United Nations security official warned that there is "potential for violence with disastrous consequences" if the election is not handled carefully.

The ongoing conflict in the state will hinder the population's participation in an election, and persistent human rights violations suggest there is no possibility of people being able to vote freely and fairly. Even if the election is to finally go ahead, South Sudan's violent and unstable environment will prevent the result from being credible.

3. Guinea-Bissau parliamentary election

24 NOVEMBER 2024

Clashes between two army factions in Guinea-Bissau in December 2023 left two people dead and caused a political crisis after President Umaro Embaló labelled it an attempted coup and dissolved the opposition-led parliament just six months after it had been elected. Security forces carried out the order with excessive force, using tear gas to block lawmakers from accessing the chamber. The original fighting was sparked by the arrest of two cabinet ministers from the African Party for the Independence of Guinea-Bissau and Cabo Verde (PAIGC) on corruption charges; PAIGC has described the president's response as unconstitutional. According to Freedom House, voters in Guinea-Bissau have a lack of free choice in the country's elections as politicians continue to be influenced by corruption, while organised crime has created an unstable political environment which significantly hinders democracy and freedom of expression. ✖

TECH WATCH

Games without frontiers

MARK STIMPSON on how video games have become a battleground in freedom of expression

BLACK MYTH: WUKONG is set to be one of the biggest gaming hits of the year after it sold more than 10 million copies in less than three days after its August launch.

The role-playing game, developed by Game Science, is inspired by the 16th century Chinese novel Journey to the West featuring an anthropomorphic monkey, also the inspiration for the hit 1970s television series Monkey. Players of the game become this staff-wielding monkey.

All standard video-game fare.

Yet concerns have been raised after gaming influencers, who have an essential role in the success or otherwise

ABOVE: Do rules over early access to hit game Black Myth: Wukong reveal the hidden hand of the censor?

of new titles, were only given access to advance copies of the game if they agreed to a number of conditions regarding their reviews of the new title. One condition was that their reviews must not mention "politics, violence, nudity, feminist propaganda, fetishisation, and other content that instigates negative discourse". It is not specified exactly what "feminist propaganda" entails.

Another rule forbade the use of "trigger words such as 'quarantine' or 'isolation' or 'Covid-19'", a sure sign that either the Chinese Communist Party was involved in drafting the rules or that the developer was self-censoring for fear of upsetting the Chinese government.

China's Global Times said that concern about the rules had led to inaccurate coverage in Western media. It wrote in an editorial that "the radar of some anti-China forces is triggered when Black Myth: Wukong is increasingly considered as a symbol of China's soft power" and specifically criticised the BBC.

It said: "Their strategy of attacking the game is just the same old Western tactic - politicising every Chinese achievement, even in the realm of gaming. What's next? Will they portray the Chinese gaming industry as a 'threat' in the future?"

China's gaming industry was worth around 300 billion yuan ($41 billion) in 2023, out of a global total of around $184 billion.

So, is the gaming sector about to become the new frontier in free expression? Possibly. The gaming sector is already double the size of the movies and entertainment sector. Messages and morals portrayed in video games are arguably as influential as those displayed in films.

It is little wonder that China, or those doing its bidding, are interested in what people have to say. ✖

Free speech in numbers

26
The number of people released as part of a prisoner swap between Russia and Western countries on 1 August

11
The number of mourners at the funeral of gifted pianist Pavel Kushnir, who died in a Russian jail after a hunger strike in protest at the invasion of Ukraine

51.2%
Share of vote claimed by Nicolas Maduro in the Venezuelan presidential election

67%
Share of vote claimed by opposition politician Edmundo González in the same election

950 million
Number of active users of messaging app Telegram, whose founder Pavel Durov was arrested in France in August

The Index

PEOPLE WATCH

DAISY RUDDOCK highlights the stories of human rights defenders under attack

Zara Esmaeili

IRAN

Women's rights activist Zara Esmaeili was arrested by Iranian security forces after a video she posted on social media of her singing Back to Black by Amy Winehouse in public without a hijab went viral. Esmaeili is known for her performances in parks and on trains, which are done in protest of the Islamic Republic's laws prohibiting women from singing, dancing and not wearing a hijab in public. Esmaeili's family has not been able to contact her since she was detained, and there is no knowledge of her whereabouts or condition.

Bakhrom Khamroev

RUSSIA

Human rights defender and lawyer Bakhrom Khamroev had his sentence upheld by a court in Russia in August. Khamroev, who was born in Uzbekistan, is well-known for providing legal defence to Muslims accused of being in the Hizb ut-Tahrir organisation, which is banned in several countries. He was arrested in 2022 and sentenced to 22 years in prison for "public calls for terrorist activities, public justification of terrorism or propaganda of terrorism" after allegedly making posts on social media about religion.

Arif Sohel

BANGLADESH

Arif Sohel, a human rights defender from Bangladesh, was placed on a six-day remand by a court in Dhaka in July. Sohel had been abducted from his home in Ambagan two days before, and his whereabouts were unknown until his court appearance. Sohel was targeted for being a key member of The Students Against Discrimination Movement - a student-led protest demanding reform of the quota system in government jobs in Bangladesh. Sohel was one of thousands detained before Prime Minister Sheikh Hasina fled the country.

Antonio Pacheco

EL SALVADOR

Five human and environmental rights activists from El Salvador including Antonio Pacheco are currently under house arrest after their public hearing - intended to take place in July - was postponed until October. Antonio Pacheco and Saul Rivas Ortega are human rights defenders in the Santa Marta area while Alejandro Laínez García, Miguel Ángel Gámez and Pedro Rivas Laínez are community leaders. They are all on trial due to unsubstantiated allegations linking them to a 1989 murder and have been under house arrest since September 2023.

Ink spot

In late August, the Taliban announced a wide-ranging new Law on the Promotion of Virtue and the Prevention of Vice which gives the state the right to control and censor people's private lives in Afghanistan.

These "vice and virtue" laws state that women must wear clothing covering their entire bodies. The rules also say women's voices must not be heard in public which includes being overheard singing or reading outside their homes.

UN Human Rights Office spokesperson Ravina Shamdasani said the new laws make women into "faceless, voiceless shadows".

The silencing of Afghan women is picked up here by Italian cartoonist Enrico Bertuccioli.

World In Focus:
Venezuela

Protests erupted in Venezuela in July after incumbent candidate Nicolás Maduro claimed victory in the presidential elections. Evidence suggests that the election was rigged and the result is hotly disputed by the opposition party

1 Caracas

The recent election results have been widely questioned, with world leaders calling for an investigation into their validity after opposition complaints about a fabricated vote count. Thousands of people took to the streets of Venezuela capital Caracas to protest the alleged corruption in the election and were met with a large police response using tear gas and rubber bullets. There were already fears of a violent crackdown due to the Maduro administration's reputation for having a heavy-handed approach to demonstrators, and these concerns escalated once the president promised to "pulverise" those challenging his rule. So far, human rights groups claim that more than 2,000 people have been arrested and at least 22 people have been killed in the election's aftermath.

2 Portuguesa

Although most of the protests occurred in the capital city, free expression issues could be found country-wide. Polling stations were a particular cause for concern, as voters were met with long queues and delays on election day, and there were reports of some voters being blocked from accessing them altogether or even stations being moved without warning. Prior to election day, Transparencia Electoral - a Venezuelan NGO - warned of irregularities in the electoral process after opposition leader Maria Corina Machado was blocked from running. Some officials who went to polling stations to observe the process were intimidated or banned from entering. Repression continued after the election; a number of opposition members were rounded up and arrested - campaign coordinator María Oropeza even livestreamed her own arrest from her home in Portuguesa.

3 Venezuela-Colombia border

Over the past 10 years there has been a surge in citizens migrating out of Venezuela due to the dire economic circumstances, with a reported 7.8 million having fled the country. This became a major talking point during the election as the government made it virtually impossible for those living abroad to vote, disenfranchising millions of people. Voters abroad faced a number of hurdles - those registering to vote had to provide a valid identity card (passports weren't allowed) which are not issued abroad. This meant many Venezuelans whose IDs had expired could not vote. Venezuelan migrants complained that they had been omitted from the electoral register altogether, and that consulates opened for voter registration at very limited times. The result of this was that fewer than 68,000 people overseas were registered to vote, despite an estimated 3.9 million Venezuelans abroad being of voting age.

The Index

MY INSPIRATION

Three knights of freedom

FRANAK VIAČORKA, chief adviser to Sviatlana Tsikhanouskaya and ex-political prisoner, writes about his heroes behind bars

LEFT: In June, opposition figure Franak Viačorka was sentenced to 20 years in prison in absentia

FOR THE PAST four years, every morning, I wake up with a feeling of pain and guilt. This guilt has become ingrained in the hearts of many active Belarusians, both in exile and within the country, ever since Lukashenka's regime began its brutal repression. Why? Because every day, more than 1,400 people are deprived of the basic joys of life, imprisoned on political grounds. They can't enjoy the summer sun, the taste of morning coffee, or the thrill of watching the historical US presidential debates. Their only joy – a short walk in a tiny prison yard, or a rare letter from a parent or child, if the censors allow it.

Among these political prisoners are people from all walks of life – Nobel laureates, pensioners, students – who were leading normal lives until Lukashenka's regime threw them in jail. But the pain cuts deepest for those I know and admire personally. These are true friends who played important roles in my life, whose voices and thoughts I miss profoundly. They are my heroes, three knights of freedom: Ales Bialiatski, Ihar Losik, and Pavel Belavus.

The regime has made him suffer beyond words

Ales was always the one who saved me. As the head of the human rights centre Viasna and later a Nobel laureate, he was more than just a leader, he was a lifeline for those crushed under Lukashenka's ruthless regime. Every time I was arrested or detained, he felt it deeply, as if it were happening to him. And when I was thrown into prison, he was the first to reach out, the first to fight for my release. I'll never forget our meeting just months before his own arrest. He told me he was going back to Minsk. I asked him if he was afraid. He looked at me, calm and resolute, and said, "What do we have to fear? Let them be afraid." They sentenced him to 10 years in prison. Ales is more than brave - he's a warrior, a knight of human rights, standing tall against the darkness.

Then there's Pavel Belavus. Pavel is the heartbeat of Belarusian culture. Even under the suffocating grip of dictatorship, he breathed life into our nation – organising festivals, massive concerts, and keeping the spirit of Belarus alive. He never flinched at bureaucracy, never backed down from rejection. He always pushed the boundaries of what seemed impossible. Because of him, countless Belarusians rediscovered their language, their history, their identity. I remember us dreaming up a T-shirt design with a traditional Belarusian ornament, something simple, yet powerful, a way for Belarusians to wear their pride. Soon, tens of thousands of people were wearing that shirt. But the regime saw his creativity, his unstoppable energy, as a threat. They locked him away for 10 years. Pavel is more than a cultural leader – he is a knight of our heritage, a guardian of our soul.

And then there's Ihar Losik, someone so close to me, someone who feels like a brother. I met Ihar more than a decade ago on Twitter [X]. His sharp wit, his fearless commentary on Belarusian politics, it was like nothing else. He spoke truth to power with a clarity that few could match. Later, he created the most influential news channels on Telegram, lifelines for so many, guiding them through the chaos of our times. But for this, the regime has made him suffer beyond words. He's been tortured, driven to the edge. He's attempted suicide more than once behind bars. For a year and a half now, they've kept him in the dark, no contact, no news, not even a word to his lawyer or family. They sentenced him to 15 years, but what they truly fear is his voice. Ihar is a knight of free speech, a beacon of hope in a world where they try to silence us.

I believe each Belarusian has someone – a friend, a family member, or even just an acquaintance – in prison. Every Belarusian feels this pain, and this guilt for them. But this pain and guilt don't stop us from fighting for them. They are not just our pain, they are also our strength. We must draw inspiration from their heroism and their dedication. They can't speak now, so we must be their voice. And we won't stop until each and every one of them is free. ✖

CREDIT: Handout

FEATURES

"If [Hillsborough] happened in the old Soviet
Union, the West would be using it as an
example of how the state failed – a massive cover-up."

A CITY'S LIMITS | FRANCIS CLARKE | P24

A vote for a level playing field

CLEMENCE MANYUKWE reports that the Mozambique elections will be a test for freedom of expression

MOZAMBIQUE IS SET to hold presidential elections on 9 October, but the credibility of the forthcoming poll is being questioned after the Democratic Alliance Coalition (CAD) was barred from taking part.

The coalition had backed the popular independent candidate Venâncio Mondlane, who is now the main challenger to the ruling Frelimo party. By issuing the ban, the government has effectively ensured that the one independent candidate who might challenge the ruling party will lack the resources and infrastructure to run a professional political campaign.

Mondlane is one of four presidential candidates approved by the Constitutional Council, Mozambique's highest body in matters of constitutional and electoral law. He is up against Daniel Chapo from Frelimo; Ossufo Momade from Renamo (up until now the main opposition party); and Lutero Simango, from the Mozambique Democratic Movement (MDM).

Mondlane is seen by many in Mozambique as the only person who can beat Chapo, who is representing the party of outgoing president Felipe Nyusi. Frelimo has been governing the country since independence from Portugal in 1975.

This is the second time Mondlane has been stripped of support. He was once a senior figure in Renamo and wanted to be its presidential candidate, but he was stopped from challenging current leader Momade during the party's congress in May.

A charismatic leader – riding on promises to deliver an honest, transparent and reformist government that will remove Mozambique from the list of the poorest countries in the world – Mondlame appeals to young people in particular.

Two thirds of the country's population of 33 million are under 25 and these increasingly highly-educated Gen Z-ers are threatening the establishment.

In an interview with Index, human rights defender Adriano Nuvunga, from Maputo's Centre for Democracy and Development, said the barring of CAD was a concerning development.

"Mozambique elections are highly exclusionary," he said. "Frelimo keeps power by excluding candidates, excluding political parties.

"Once you have an electoral system and electoral management that excludes candidates and excludes political parties from contesting elections, clearly you do not have a level playing field for electoral competition. It's restricted. Government only allows those competitors that do not represent a significant challenge to the incumbent."

Nuvunga said it was all part of an "opaque, non-transparent and fraudulent electoral system that is meant to perpetuate the status quo in the country".

The October election comes amid a long-running unresolved conflict between the government and a radical Islamist group in Cabo Delgado, northern Mozambique, which has been going on since 2017.

One of the important tasks facing the next president will be to come up with new strategies to restore security there as Nyusi's route of relying simply on a military response has failed to yield results.

He has rejected dialogue with insurgents and failed to address factors that have made the province a fertile recruitment ground for the terror group. A strategy to contain extremism that was crafted with support from the World Bank and the European Union, which identified poverty and social inequality as drivers of radicalisation, has not been acted on by the president, who has also failed to come up with development policies.

Tomás Queface, an analyst at Cabo Ligado Observatory, told Index that the fact that Frelimo had chosen a young presidential candidate – Chapo is 47, and would be the first president born after the country's independence in 1975 – did not mean that change was on the horizon and Chapo would just continue Nyusi's policies.

On the other hand, he added that Mondlane had shown that he was not someone who blindly followed the directives of his party but who thought independently. More importantly, he has shared his manifesto which, instead of just making promises, proposes reforms to electoral law and changes to the management of natural resources and other sectors which would return more power to ordinary people.

He added that the majority of Mozambique's population had lost trust in the election process because of fraud and irregularities. During the last election, he claimed, the results from

ABOVE: Mozambique's President Filipe Nyusi (L), also the party chief of the ruling party Frelimo, congratulates Daniel Franciso Chapo for becoming Frelimo's candidate in the presidential election in October

RIGHT: Camp for displaced people in Cabo Delgado in northern Mozambique

polling stations in Maputo were changed – either by the electoral commission or the Constitutional Council.

Responding to the rigging allegations, in his state of the nation address in December, Nyusi said they were just "isolated irregularities".

He added that "in no country in the world is democracy perfect".

However, Queface said there were many more problems in the country.

"Because the rate of unemployment is very high, the cost of living is unaffordable for the majority [and] public servant sectors are on strike because of poor working and salary conditions," he said. "Young people have no hope because they have to bribe people for the few jobs available. After 49 years of independence, Mozambique remains one of the poorest countries in the world. Politicians are very detached from reality. People want an alternative to Frelimo."

He also said that Cabo Delgado was an enormous election issue and that the government had failed to guarantee the safety of people there, instead making a huge effort to close the province to journalists and researchers.

Terrorist groups have been committing acts of barbarity there, including beheadings, forced disappearances and kidnappings.

Queface said several journalists had been threatened, arrested and killed by Mozambican security forces for reporting on the conflict.

"The province represents a risk zone for journalists and researchers," he said. "Ibrahimo Abu Mbaruco, a journalist who was based in the district of Palma, was allegedly kidnapped in 2020 by the military and his whereabouts are still

unknown. Amade Abubacar, a journalist based in Macomia, was arrested by the authorities – allegedly for collaborating with terrorists, something that has never been proven."

Khanyo Farise, Amnesty International's deputy regional director for East and Southern Africa, backed Queface's claims.

"Authorities have so far failed to investigate the killing of newspaper editor Joao Fernando Chamusse and the enforced disappearance of Mbaruco in the Cabo Delgado region," he said.

Social activist and human rights defender Abudo Gafuro Manana told Index that elections have a history of worsening human rights violations in his country, in particular around issues such as the conflict in Cabo Delgado, with research on such issues violently prohibited.

"People are not free to speak. There is a lot of censorship at all levels," he said. "I have already received three threats for talking about the Cabo Delgado conflict.

"I have opened two cases with the prosecutor's office [but] I have never received a response to the threats I received.

"Freedom of expression is far from being a constitutional right for Mozambicans in general – and especially here in Cabo Delgado."

In June, the International Republican Institute (IRI) convened a private roundtable discussion on Mozambique, focusing on the elections and how the US government could support the country diplomatically and through programmes including a 10-year strategy to prevent conflict and promote stability.

The participants called for international actors to amplify what citizen observers, civil society, journalists and others on the ground are doing and to identify and engage influential stakeholders who have the capacity to choose violence or non-violence and escalation or de-escalation.

International pressure can help. Farise said that after Amnesty International published a report into the conflict highlighting war crimes that the mercenary Dyck Advisory Group allegedly committed on behalf of the state, the group was sent back to South Africa.

"That is a measure of accountability, though not the legal process we would prefer." ✖

Clemence Manyukwe is a freelance journalist based in Zimbabwe

53(03):12/13|DOI:10.1177/03064220241285655

These increasingly highly educated Gen Z-ers are threatening the establishment

CREDIT: (Nyusi & Chapo) Constancio Sitoe/Xinhua/Alamy; MAXPPP/Alamy

Whistling the tune of 'terrorism'

NEDIM TÜRFENT examines the increasingly violent suppression of Kurdish language and culture in Turkey

RAMAZAN ŞIMŞEK ANNOUNCED that the café he runs in the main Kurdish city of Diyarbakır would serve its guests only in Kurdish starting on 15 May.

It was an act of defiance which was quickly punished.

He was detained by Turkish police on charges of "terrorist propaganda" and was placed under house arrest and banned from leaving Turkey.

Kurds have been celebrating 15 May as *Cejna Zimanê Kurdî* (Kurdish Language Day) for almost 20 years. It is the day the magazine Hawar was first published in Damascus in 1932, under the leadership of Kurdish linguist Celadet Alî Bedirxan.

But the Kurdish language has faced significant challenges since that time.

From the 1920s to the 1980s, Turkey officially denied the existence of the language and referred to Kurds as "mountain Turks".

Names of cities, towns and villages were changed to Turkish in the 1940s, the language banned and fines imposed for every word spoken on the street.

There was an easing-off for a while and then following the military coup on 12 September 1980 things became worse again. Kurdish was officially banned in both public and private – and anyone who spoke, sang or broadcast in Kurdish was arrested and imprisoned.

It was only in the early 2000s, as part of the EU accession process (which was never completed), that Turkey took steps to allow the language to be spoken freely.

Although this created an expectation of democratisation, hopes were exhausted when the peace process with the Kurds ended in 2013. After this, Kurdish culture, art, literature and

language were severely curtailed again.

Kurdish journalist Ferîd Demîrel points out the recent increase in attacks on Kurds.

"Many people have been attacked for speaking Kurdish on the streets," he said. "Concerts have been banned [and] artists detained. Writers' events have been cancelled and Kurdish media outlets either shut down or blocked."

During the 2016 state of emergency, following another coup attempt, Kurdish news outlets and magazines were shut down and associations working on Kurdish language and culture closed.

Azadiya Welat, the only Kurdish daily newspaper in Turkey, was closed down.

ABOVE: A man reads the Kurdish newspaper Azadiya Welat in Diyarbakır, Turkey in 2009. By 2016 the paper had been closed down. Now there are no daily newspapers available in Kurdish

Mehmet Alî Ertaş, editor-in-chief of the weekly Kurdish newspaper Xwebûn, highlights that there are still no daily Kurdish newspapers in Turkey.

Ertaş, who has been working for Kurdish newspapers and agencies for 21 years, said: "Since July [2024], there have been restrictions on the Kurdish language in various areas in Turkey. Kurdish hostility is heading toward a dangerous point."

Dozens of people who danced to the

The government sees the existence of Kurdish as a threat in every field

accompaniment of Kurdish songs were arrested this summer. In the Kurdish city of Siirt, three sisters were arrested for performing *halay* at a wedding, and their mother was placed under house arrest.

Four artists who sang songs at a wedding in Hakkari were also arrested. Operations were carried out in different cities, but the accusation was the same: "propagandising a terrorist organisation".

The *halay* (*govend* in Kurdish) is a folk dance which takes many different forms and is popular among Kurds. Artist Baran Bozyel told Index that targeting *halay* is unreasonable and aimed at assimilation.

She added: "Despite the pressures, we'll continue to sing our songs and be the voice of our people. As artists, we give struggle to contribute to the cultural creation of Kurdish identity."

Ironically, the government has opened a television channel called TRT Kurdî – but only to propagate its ideology, using the Kurdish language as a tool for its propaganda efforts.

When Kurds themselves use their language in daily life, or to protect their culture and identity, they are subjected to various bans and restrictions.

Since the end of July, the authorities have removed the *Pêşî Peya* (Pedestrians First) traffic warning signs on roads in Kurdish cities. Such restrictions on the use of Kurdish in public spaces are evident in various locations, ranging from prisons to hospitals.

Although there is no official ban on Kurdish today, when MPs speak it in the Turkish parliament, their microphones are switched off and Kurdish is recorded as an "unknown language".

Authorities cite the third article of the constitution as the reason for the switch-off: "The Turkish state is indivisible with its country and nation. Its language is Turkish." In 2009, when

then US President Barack Obama spoke English in the Turkish parliament, his microphone was not turned off. Similarly, the microphone isn't switched off when Arabic is spoken. The main issue appears to be enmity against Kurds.

This hostility is also evident in education, as millions of Kurdish children in Turkey are unable to receive education in their mother tongue. Prohibited as a language of education, Kurdish is allowed only as an "elective course" in select schools.

Omer Fîdan, co-president of Kurdish PEN, highlights the prohibition on Kurdish education.

"This ban undermines the basis of all Kurdish studies, literature and storytelling," he said. "This is a direct barrier. Without Kurdish education, there will be no readers. If there are no readers, it is not possible for storytellers to reach society."

Many people aren't even aware of the existence of Kurdish works – but the Turkish state follows every word. Kurdish theatre and concerts are other media that agitate the authorities.

Bêrû, the Kurdish adaptation of Dario Fo's satirical play Trumpets and

Raspberries, faced numerous bans citing "public safety". In contrast, the Turkish adaptation faced no bans.

Labelling the bans on Kurdish theatre as a fascist practice, actress Sakîna Jîr, of the Teatra Jîyana Nû theatre group, said: "The government sees the existence of Kurdish as a threat in every field – from theatre to music. But we won't give up, because the existence of language is indispensable for the survival of a people's culture and identity. Practising arts in the mother tongue leads people to search for an identity."

Although the government of President Recep Tayyip Erdoğan claims to have lifted the long-recurring ban on Kurdish, its actions suggest otherwise.

Journalist and writer Musa Anter was detained and tortured by police 81 years ago for "whistling in Kurdish".

It is not known whether this escalating hostility towards the language will return to such a point, but this course of events raises an eerie curiosity. ✖

Nedim Türfent is a Kurdish journalist based in Germany

53(03):14/15|DOI:10.1177/03064220241285656

RIGHT: Young Kurdish men and women taking part in a traditional *halay* dance at a wedding in Mardin, Turkey. The dance is now banned

Running low on everything

AMY BOOTH looks at how Bolivian journalists bear the brunt of the country's pain as the economic situation looks increasingly bleak

ON THE AFTERNOON of 26 June 2024, Bolivian troops marched through the streets of La Paz and rammed the door to the presidential palace with tankettes – small tanks the size of cars – forcing their way inside.

President Luis Arce stormed downstairs to face off with disgraced general Juan José Zúñiga and ordered him to stand down, before abruptly swearing in a new military high command who ordered the troops to fall back. They complied. An attempted military coup had, it seemed, been put down in time for tea.

Outside, Zúñiga was arrested – but not before declaring to the watching press that he had been ordered to stage the uprising by the president who wanted to boost his popularity.

The episode paints a dismaying picture of democratic fragility ahead of the presidential elections in August 2025 – and an adverse scenario for journalists, NGOs and other critical voices navigating polarisation, stigmatisation and physical violence.

Journalists covering the crisis were tear-gassed and manhandled by the security forces and insulted by pro-government protesters as they tried to work. Three weeks later, they received an invitation from the Ministry of Government to attend a working breakfast. Reporters were quick to denounce it as a government attempt to lean on them to glean information that supported the official narrative.

When it comes to rights and freedoms, economic, party-political and institutional factors all pose threats to

LEFT: Bolivian President Luis Arce raises a defiant clenched fist in La Paz after an attempted coup

press freedom, freedom of expression and the right to freedom of assembly.

The 26 June attack was particularly disturbing because it carried echoes of the crisis that forced former president Evo Morales from office in November 2019.

After controversial electoral fraud accusations against Morales sparked a wave of lethal protests, the police mutinied, and the army "suggested" Morales step down – in what many decried as a coup. Bolivia was ruled for a year by the caretaker government of former far-right senator Jeanine Áñez before Arce was elected.

Some 37 people were killed during the crisis, and there were attacks on the press all over the country, with journalists suffering physical attacks and having their offices and equipment destroyed and burned. The security forces as well as protesters and partisan shock groups were behind the violence.

The Inter-American Commission on Human Rights declared in a report on the state of human rights in the country that "never before had it been so difficult to exercise journalism in Bolivia", and recommended that a non-state organisation be established to offer legal and psychological support to at-risk journalists. Almost five years later, this has not happened.

Landlocked and sparsely populated, Bolivia has long been one of the poorest and least-developed countries in South America. However, for the past two decades, it has enjoyed a cycle of economic prosperity, as high prices for its gas exports bolstered state coffers.

The left-wing government of Morales and his Movement Towards Socialism (MAS) party ploughed the proceeds into social programmes that helped cut poverty and tackle inequality.

Now, the model is becoming unsustainable. The country's gas reserves are running out – a large discovery

in July notwithstanding – and the government has been unable to coax a profit from the country's enormous lithium deposits.

Now, Bolivia's international reserves are running on empty, making it increasingly onerous to pay for imports and subsidies on items such as fuel.

At the time of writing, the boliviano is trading at more than 10 to the dollar in parallel exchange markets while at home it has been pegged by the government at just seven to the dollar for more than a decade.

Miguel Miranda, co-ordinator of the human rights incidence team at the Bolivian NGO CEDIB, which seeks to archive history and build knowledge for the future, told Index that cuts were inevitable. "It will hit the popular classes the hardest," he said. "So how are they [the government] going to contain that? Because people will hit the streets. [They will respond] with measures that restrict rights."

Miranda also fears the government will try to ward off possible protests by passing decrees that could be used to restrict them.

But protests are not the only prospective casualty in such a scenario. Strapped for cash, the government has turned heavily towards harmful extractive industries – and environmentalists sounding the alarm have had a chilly reception.

In May 2023, the senate passed a law allowing the government to trade gold bought from local mining co-operatives. Yet, indigenous people and park rangers have accused gold miners of illegally pushing into national parks, polluting rivers and violently crushing resistance. Indigenous communities and environmental groups have also raised concerns over projects such as the Chepete and Bala megadams, which

would allow Bolivia to export power, but which would flood large tracts of biodiverse protected areas.

Many young, grassroots environmental organisations enjoy such social legitimacy that governments baulk at the political cost of moving against them, Miranda argued. Although some of the region's most repressive regimes – such as the government in Nicaragua run by Daniel Ortega – have done so anyway, Arce has not displayed this kind of authoritarianism.

"They're a stone in the government's shoe, because they have a strong moral value," Miranda said.

Arce's challenges as election season looms are not only economic. Barely had he got his feet under the table as president when cracks started to emerge between him and his erstwhile mentor, Morales. Today, their MAS party is experiencing a full-blown feud so bitter that a party conference decided to expel Arce and his vice-president David Choquehuanca in October 2023.

The split is affecting journalists. On 10 July, a reporter from the pro-Morales station Radio Kawsachun Coca was in La Paz to cover a multi-party meeting convened by the electoral authorities. She was attacked by Arce supporters who set off firecrackers, pushed her, threw stones and other objects at her and chanted: "Out! Out! Out!"

In a joint statement, Bolivia's National Association of Journalists and the La Paz Journalists' Association condemned the attack, noting that it was not the first time the political divide had sparked violence against journalists.

"This lamentable incident adds to a series of grave violations of freedom of expression and of the press, which are encouraged by stigmatising discourse that incites violence against journalists," they warned. "Once again, this leaves →

 They're a stone in the government's shoe, because they have a strong moral value

CREDIT: AP Photo/Juan Karita/Alamy

LEFT: Journalists from the Federation of Press Workers protest against further press regulation

→ evident the negligence of the authorities, who are called on to guarantee the safety of journalists and press workers as they carry out their jobs."

While in government, Morales frequently accused critical media outlets of lying, and Reporters Without Borders has warned that there is a "trivialisation of stigmatisation" of journalists. The country slid by seven places to 124/180 in the organisation's 2024 World Press Freedom Index.

Unitas, a non-profit that monitors rights and freedoms in Bolivia, identified 143 cases of press freedom violations during 2023. Of these, 30 were physical, sexual or psychological attacks against journalists, while 28 involved threats or intimidation. All too often, these attacks go unpunished.

In one of the most egregious incidents of recent years, six journalists reporting on a land occupation in Guarayos, in the eastern Santa Cruz department, were met by men with guns, who shot their vehicles' wheels, kidnapped them and destroyed some of their equipment.

Bolivian police played the attack down, describing it as an "altercation". Nobody has been prosecuted for the attack and Zulema Alanes, president of the National Association of Journalists of Bolivia, warns that upcoming judicial deadlines mean it could soon end in impunity.

Claudia Teran, co-ordinator of Unitas's rights defenders programme, pointed out that while attacks were often perpetrated by private individuals or shock groups, who may or may not have ties to the government, the government did little to protect the journalists affected. "When journalists report this kind of attack, the state's mechanisms of investigation and punishment are very weak," she said.

Even for routine coverage of street protests, insults and aggression against journalists have become commonplace, according to Alanes. Women are particular targets for sexual harassment and degrading insults. "They say, 'Why don't you go back to the kitchen?'" Alanes said. "We're in a situation of violence and persistent violation of press

freedom and of direct physical violence against journalists, with impunity and without reparations or justice."

The government also uses state advertising spending as a mechanism to discipline media outlets. In June 2023, government-critical newspaper Pagina Siete announced its closure. In a letter to readers, president of the board Raúl Garáfulic Lehm blamed a perfect storm, accusing the government of withholding state advertising and harassing the paper with audits and fines, while going easy on more sympathetic outlets. One of the major challenges likely to face journalists going into the elections is a scenario of extreme polarisation, Zulema Alanes of the National Association of Journalists said. It and other civil society organisations have formulated recommendations to guarantee that citizens can inform themselves. One of these involves organising obligatory debates for presidential candidates. They have also recommended that Bolivia's electoral authorities ally with fact-checking organisations Chequea Bolivia and Bolivia Verifica to combat the spread of misinformation and fake news.

Claudia Teran, of Unitas, and Alanes both called for Bolivia to implement a law on access to information. "Access to public information should be the rule, not the exception, and refusal should be justified," Teran said.

For Miranda, Bolivia doesn't just need policies. It needs a paradigm shift.

"We need a society that really enjoys the right to freedom of information," he said. "We need to move towards critical dissidence, towards a vigorous critical citizenship that permits structural change." ✖

Amy Booth is a journalist reporting from South America

We're in a situation of violence and persistent violation of press freedom

53(03):16/18|DOI:10.1177/03064220241285682

A dictatorship in the making

A clampdown on protests could lead to a return to dictatorship in Kenya.
ROBERT KITUYI reports on how state violence is increasing

A HARD KNOCK TO the side of the head can silence a journalist and shut down an entire newsroom.

John Kituyi, the owner and editor of Kenya's Weekly Mirror – and my uncle – fell victim to a fatal blow that silenced him forever by a gang on a motorbike near his Eldoret home in April 2015. The assault, which happened 500 metres from his home after a long day editing, led to the closure of his publication and scattered his team.

We had worked together for about five years before his untimely death. His attackers stole his phone and office keys but left his wallet and an expensive watch.

He was targeted because of our investigation into the disappearance of key witnesses, including Meshack Yebei, who were sought by the International Criminal Court (ICC) for alleged prosecution witness interference in 2007 post-election violence. Threats against our team intensified after my uncle refused to abandon his investigation.

The shadow of those who bludgeoned him to death continue to cast a dark

ABOVE: Journalists protesting in Nakuru, Kenya after one of their colleagues was shot in July 2024

cloud over Kenyan journalists. They face threats including harassment, intimidation and the risk of being hit by live bullets while reporting on protests.

President William Ruto now appears to have adopted a policy of even more heavy-handedness against the media and critical voices.

Janak Oloo, a veteran journalist and director of programmes with the ➔

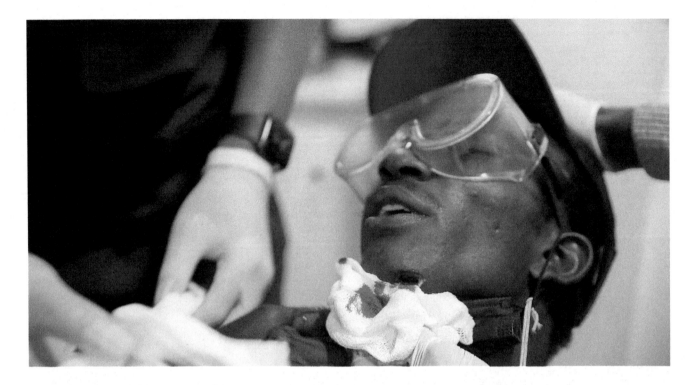

ABOVE: A protester receives medical treatment from a team of paramedics in Nairobi in July 2024 after he was hit by a tear-gas canister during a demonstration against police violence

→ Kenya Correspondents Association, draws a comparison between the current situation in Kenya and the period under president Daniel arap Moi in the 1990s, particularly regarding press freedom and expression.

He notes that the Ruto regime has demonstrated "even greater repression" since he took power in 2022 – the year I was forced to leave the country because of my reporting into human rights abuses.

Despite the constraints of a progressive constitution and the judiciary, Oloo highlights attempts to "gag the press through negative rhetoric", citing official warnings – such as a recent letter from the Communication Authority to Nation Media Group, which cautioned media houses that some content on the protests violated the country's constitutional limits on freedom of expression, as well as "brazen attacks on journalists during protests".

Oloo also emphasises that "abductions and killings are as chilling as during Moi's era". Under Moi detainees could be produced in court on trumped-up charges, but now "many are found dead under suspicious circumstances".

He contends that the situation would be even worse without a strong constitution, responsive judiciary and social media.

Independent media outlets with national coverage – among them Citizen Television of Royal Media Services, Nation Media Group, and Standard Group – have also faced online threats in what appears to be a well co-ordinated effort to silence or censor their reporting.

The president has accused both international and local organisations of financing and inciting nationwide protests against his administration and has condemned the media for "glorifying" the protests that began on 18 June, sparked by a controversial proposed tax increase.

The protests, driven mainly by young Kenyans, were a culmination of deep frustration over soaring living costs, bad governance, rampant corruption, rising national debt and a series of unfulfilled government promises.

Protests spread to about half of Kenya's 47 counties, driven initially by opposition to a taxation bill which was withdrawn after demonstrators stormed and set parts of the parliament building on fire on 25 June.

Officers indiscriminately fired tear gas and water cannons and used rubber and live bullets to attack unarmed protesters, especially those with recording devices.

The youth-led movement alleges that it was infiltrated by government agents, who exploited the movement's leaderless and non-tribal stance

Several journalists and bloggers recounted brutal assaults on protesters, with those abducted saying they have been tortured to extract information about organisers and funders.

Catherine Wanjeri Kariuki and Macharia Gaitho were prominent media victims. On 16 July, Kariuki, a Media Max journalist, was shot three times by police in Nakuru County while covering protests, despite wearing a marked Press jacket.

The day after, veteran journalist Gaitho was abducted from a police station where he had sought protection. He was handcuffed, driven away and released only after public outrage following an online viral video of his abduction.

Meanwhile, CNN photojournalist Fabien Muhure faced harassment and was hit with water cannons by police during the protests.

According to press freedom groups including Article 19, the Kenya Editors Guild and the Media Council of Kenya, at least 18 journalists have been physically attacked, harassed or intimidated. Five more have been arrested, and there have been six documented cases of equipment being damaged or confiscated.

The initial street protests ceased in August because of the government's brutal crackdown. However, the movement has shifted online, where protesters are now targeting specific institutions they perceive as weak links in their demands for better governance, adherence to the rule of law, and an end to corruption. But their campaigns are also being countered online.

Some key protesters, including Godfrey Masasa, accused the president's online army of targeting, coercing, or incentivising prominent social media influencers central to the movement's digital lifeline. The youth-led movement alleges that it was infiltrated by government agents, who exploited the movement's leaderless and non-tribal stance. State-sponsored bloggers launched hashtags like #CrushAnarchists, particularly targeting

CREDIT: SOPA Images Limited/Alamy

This alarming situation in Kenya has raised serious concerns both within the country and internationally

those who resisted co-option or compromise by government operatives.

This strategy aimed to fracture the movement particularly on X—a key platform for real-time coordination of nationwide protests. Posts sought to undermine the protests' legitimacy, erode public trust in their message, and reinforce the state's narrative as having "addressed all the protesters' demands".

In a move seen as an attempt to quell dissatisfaction and consolidate legitimacy, Ruto has also reconstituted a "broad-based and inclusive government" with his long-time rival, opposition leader Raila Odinga. This tactic has been perceived as a strategy not only to weaken any meaningful opposition but also to solidify Ruto's administration amid the unrest.

Nevertheless, Kenya's civil and political rights, once a hallmark of its democratic identity, are under threat. Freedoms to protest, speak freely, and assemble are increasingly restricted, with Parliament considering laws imposing hefty fines on protesters.

Demonstrators are still facing arbitrary arrests on vague charges like "incitement" or "illegal assembly," while activists and opposition leaders are regularly targeted. Human rights NGOs are also still facing heightened scrutiny, with some being shut down due to bureaucratic obstacles and targeted harassment.

The Kenya National Commission on Human Rights (KNCHR) reports that at least 66 people are thought to have been abducted or are still missing since the protests began. The KNCHR states that at least 60 people have been killed, 601 injured, and 1,376 arrested during the protests. Some of those declared missing have resurfaced alive, while others have been found dead.

The Independent Policing Oversight Authority (IPOA) is investigating allegations of police involvement in the disappearances but has yet to provide specific details.

Meanwhile, President Ruto continues to dismiss claims of abductions, stating during a town hall meeting on 28 July in Mombasa, "If there is any Kenyan who has disappeared, I want people to step forward and say Kenyan so-and-so has disappeared. I will be very happy to deal with it."

Morris Odhiambo, Executive Director at the Centre for Law and Research International, told Index that Kenyan regimes have historically relied on brutality and manipulation – including exploiting ethnic identities – to retain power. When these tactics fail, they resort to "patronage and co-option".

The alarming situation in Kenya has raised serious concerns both within the country and internationally. Human rights groups and foreign missions, including in the USA, are sounding the alarm.

In a joint statement, 38 national and international civil society organisations have condemned "alarming and unprecedented" violent crackdowns, abductions and disappearances targeting journalists, media houses, bloggers and protesters.

Oloo warns that it will get worse for the media, too. Unlike Moi, who "made no pretence about respecting press freedom", the current regime, he told Index, "professes respect for it while violating it with abandon". ✖

Robert Kituyi is a Kenyan journalist who lives in exile in Europe

53(03):19/21|DOI:10.1177/0306422024 1285683

Leave nobody in silence

Activist **JANA PALIASHCHUK** writes about the importance of talking about Belarus's political prisoners and sending them postcards

SIX POLITICAL PRISONERS died behind bars in Belarus in the last four years. Around 250 others are suffering from critical health conditions – epilepsy, end-stage diabetes, brain tumours and other cancers. They receive little medical treatment and are often denied parcels with medicines. Those who do not "surrender" to inhumane and degrading treatment face beatings, forced psychiatric evaluations and weeks in isolation cells. Some receive new criminal charges just before they are due to be released.

People with short sentences are coerced into writing letters to Belarus president Aliaksandr Lukashenka begging for a pardon.

For anyone coming from a democratic, free country, the stories of repression are confusing because, on paper, Belarus looks as if it might be similar to theirs.

Belarus has a constitution but in 2020, Lukashenka said: "Our constitution is not written for women."

Belarus has laws, but as Lukashenka remarked: "Sometimes there's no time for laws."

Belarus calls itself a democracy, but in his address to protesting factory workers after the 2020 presidential election, Lukashenka declared: "Until you kill me, there will be no new elections."

Lukashenka takes the peaceful resistance of the Belarusian people personally, viewing any citizen inclined towards democracy and freedom as an enemy. Politicians, journalists, analysts, activists, and human rights defenders are either sentenced to years in prison or forced into exile.

Tens of thousands of ordinary people have faced repression for actions such as participating in peaceful rallies in 2020, posting historical national symbols on social media (Lukashenka despises everything Belarusian about Belarusians), or for donating via Facebook to Belarusian military volunteers fighting for Ukraine. Everything is punished – just pick your poison.

Everything is punished – just pick your poison

ABOVE: Belarus opposition activists Maria Kalesnikava (right) and Maksim Znak at a court hearing in Minsk in 2021. They have not been heard from for more than a year

The most troubling aspect of political imprisonment is when it's not even possible to ascertain if some individuals are alive. How can this happen in Europe in 2024? Easily, it turns out.

Prisoners are denied basic rights based on the "damage" they have done to the regime and Lukashenka's ego. They are cut off from legal support: no meetings with lawyers are allowed and prominent lawyers are disbarred. They are cut off from love as no phone calls or family visits are permitted. Parcels and letters often do not reach them.

They have no access to independent newspapers or TV in prison. Instead, they are forced to watch state propaganda channels that distort every bit of information. This is deprivation of contact with the outside world.

CREDIT: (courtroom) Associated Press/Alamy ; (portrait) SOPA Images Ltd/Alamy

Many "politicals", as political prisoners are often called, are not allowed to talk to other prisoners, especially if they spend weeks in punishment or solitary cells. It's easy to spot them – their uniforms are marked with yellow tags.

Often, we hear about famous repressed Belarusians only when other prisoners have served their sentences, are evacuated from the country and share what they have seen.

The final step is to forbid any correspondence – the last key in this artfully orchestrated symphony of silence. The incommunicado mode.

Blogger and political activist Siarhei Tsikhanouski, husband of Sviatlana Tsikhanouskaya, who stood against Lukashenka after the authorities refused to register him as a candidate in the 2020 elections, was sentenced to 19-and-a-half years in prison and has been in incommunicado for more than 570 days.

Musician and activist Maria Kalesnikava was sentenced to 11 years and has been in incommunicado for more than 590 days. Lawyer Maksim Znak was sentenced to 10 years and has been incommunicado for more than 600 days. The lack of news about them often compels us to ask: do we really know if they are alive?

Lukashenka practised the forced "disappearance" of his political opponents at the start of his dictatorial career. Politician Viktar Hanchar, businessman Anatol Krasouski, former interior minister Yury Zakharanka and journalist Dzmitry Zavadski all disappeared between 1999 and 2000 and are believed to have been killed on his orders. The scale of revenge is high, and now the opponents are literal hostages.

Let me be direct. People are left in survival mode. But this does not mean we cannot do anything for the safety

RIGHT: Belarus opposition leader Sviatlana Tsikhanouskaya holds a portrait of her husband, Siarhei Tsikhanouski during a press conference in Poland in 2024

The final step is to forbid any correspondence

and freedom of these political prisoners. International pressure on the regime, in various forms, proves to be at least tangible and most stressful for the autocratic ruler in Minsk.

When there was a worldwide wave of rumours questioning Tsikhanouski's condition, he was shown in rare prison footage. He had changed to the point where he was almost unrecognisable to his own wife, but we all saw him.

After Kalesnikava was moved from prison to intensive care for surgery, she was allowed a visit from her father while recovering. Propaganda didn't hesitate to show her in the hospital, so the international "hysteria" asking "Where is our Masha?" could end. It was too loud, too annoying, too unnerving for the regime.

The narrative used against hostages is that they are forgotten – by the world, families and friends. This is never true.

But if we are not allowed to reach out to them with letters of support and postcards, we can continue talking about them.

We can share their inspiring stories on social media or publish their words or artwork – as Index does with the Letters from Lukashenka's Prisoners project.

We can tell our friends about the situation in Belarus and write letters and postcards to all prisoners – including those being held incommunicado so the regime sees we haven't forgotten them, so their jailers cannot lie to them, so censors in prison never have enough black ink to cross out our loud words of solidarity, so no one is left in silence. ✖

Jana Paliashchuk is a Belarusian media expert and activist in exile. She is a researcher on Index's Letters from Lukashenka's Prisoners project

53(03):22/23|DOI:10.1177/03064220241285684

A city's limits

FRANCIS CLARKE explores a clash between local sensitivities and a cancelled event in Liverpool

BROADCASTER, AUTHOR AND political commentator Iain Dale has taken to a Liverpool stage twice in as many years, both times coinciding with the annual Labour Party Conference.

At the time of writing, it won't become a hat-trick of appearances.

Dale was due to appear for the first time at the Liverpool Philharmonic Hall on 22 September, co-hosting the For The Many live podcast. However, in July, after a blitz of social media protest, the venue cancelled the event.

"I saw somebody on Twitter [X] had an agenda towards me, but it hadn't spread like wildfire, so I didn't think anything of it," Dale told Index. "Then, literally a few hours later, my promoter called saying the Liverpool show was cancelled."

The post focused on Dale's link to Sir Norman Bettison, the former chief constable of Merseyside. As managing director of Biteback Publishing, in 2016 Dale acquired the rights to Bettison's book, Hillsborough Untold, which centred on the Hillsborough stadium disaster of April 1989 – a fatal crush at a football match in Sheffield.

As a result of the disaster, 97 fans of Liverpool Football Club died. An independent panel in 2012 showed that the crush was not the fault of the fans, and an inquest absolved them of all blame in 2016. It was ruled fans were unlawfully killed, with the police largely to blame for the disaster (though no one was prosecuted for the deaths).

Bettison is held in disdain in Liverpool after previously being accused in parliament of smearing Liverpool fans as part of a "black propaganda" campaign, aiming to shift the disaster's cause away from police and towards the fans. Bettison denies the claims.

In 2017, he was charged with four counts of misconduct in a public office for statements he was alleged to have made about Hillsborough and his role in its aftermath, which the Crown Prosecution Service claimed were untrue. All charges were dropped in 2018.

Dale told Index that money was barely a factor in the decision to publish.

"If I think there's a case to publish a book, I'll happily stand by it. Nobody has to buy it," he said. "But what cancelling an event does is deny free choice. Nobody was forced to buy a ticket."

The Liverpool Philharmonic declined to speak to Index, but in a statement made at the time it said: "Liverpool Philharmonic has made the decision that the event is not appropriate due to local sensitivities. We value the trust and support of our community and take our responsibility to uphold our shared values seriously."

When it comes to freedom of speech, should there be consideration for how it might relate to sensitive local issues?

"That was the excuse the venue used," said Dale, who recently attempted to become a Conservative candidate for parliament before withdrawing.

"If you take that to its logical extent you can make an argument for many events being cancelled due to local sensitivities.

"If somebody says something you take exception to or disagree with, the way to get over that is to argue the case

with them, and you might even change their mind."

Dale also downplayed the number of calls for cancellation on X.

"It was about two people who had support from about 10 others with large followings, so it was a complete kneejerk reaction from the Philharmonic Hall. I think in the long term they might regret it because they have set a precedent now," he said.

Simon Hughes is a Liverpool-based football writer for The Athletic. He is the author of books covering Liverpool FC

I think in the long term they might regret it because they have set a precedent now

CREDIT: News Images Ltd/Alamy

and the modern social history of the city.

He told Index that people outside the city might struggle to understand the strong, unresolved feelings that Hillsborough still elicits there.

"It's still the worst stadium disaster in Britain and people are still rightly angry about it 35 years later," he said.

"If it happened in the old Soviet Union, the West would be using it as an example of how the state failed – a massive cover-up. We have all the answers in the full public glare, yet nobody has properly been held accountable, which makes it unique."

Hughes remembers the release of Bettison's book, and thinks Dale has underestimated the depth of people's feelings in Liverpool at the time.

However, he isn't a fan of "cancel culture" more broadly, and believes it's up to people if they wish to attend.

"People might actually turn up to protest instead," he said.

"It's like when The Sun newspaper was boycotted in Liverpool. The boycott came after the paper printed falsehoods about Liverpool fans at Hillsborough

ABOVE: Liverpool FC supporters encourage a boycott of The Sun newspaper following its coverage of the Hillsborough disaster

[and] people just stopped buying it. It was a very organic decision.

"As a reporter, I want to see a free press, and if people don't believe in that press then it's a decision for them to make." ✖

Francis Clarke is a journalist and a former Tim Hetherington Fellow

53(03):24/25|DOI:10.1177/03064220241285685

History on the cutting room floor

THIỆN VIỆT explores the whims of the Vietnamese censor and the silencing of the country's history

ABOVE: Robert Downey Jr. and Hoa Xuande in The Sympathizer

HBO MAX RECENTLY showed the first episodes of The Sympathizer, a seven-part espionage thriller portraying the Vietnam War and its aftermath which was co-created by South Korean director Park Chan-wook and Don McKellar. It features Oscar-winning actor Robert Downey Jr.

The series is adapted from the Pulitzer Prize-winning novel of the same name by Vietnamese American author Việt Thanh Nguyễn, who went to the USA as a refugee. Much of the dialogue in the series is delivered in Vietnamese, although it was intended for American audiences.

While the series was partly set in Saigon (now Ho Chi Minh City), it was actually filmed in Thailand as a licence to film in Vietnam was not granted.

The book has not been translated into Vietnamese, either.

Its author wrote with heavy irony on Threads: "The Sympathizer is not officially available in Vietnamese as a novel or TV series, but my Vietnamese people have not disappointed me. I have downloaded the first six episodes [of the series] with Vietnamese subtitles, the pirated unsanctioned Vietnamese translation of the novel, and the audiobook of that translation in Vietnamese, all found on Reddit."

While the Vietnamese authorities have not said why a licence was not granted for either the filming of the movie or the translation of Nguyễn's book, its censorship is not surprising. The Sympathizer describes the Vietnam War and is written by a diasporic author who fled the regime. It is not in line with the Communist Party of Vietnam-authorised version of events.

Moreover, it falls foul of a new law on cinematography which came into force on 1 January 2023 and covers both films distributed online and foreign productions operating in Vietnam. Its catch-all Article 9 prohibits the dissemination of contents that oppose the Socialist Republic of Vietnam and anything which sabotages the great national unity bloc; damages the interests of Vietnam, its people and cultural values; and insults the national flag, the CPV flag, the national emblem or the national anthem.

This law can be interpreted widely, according to the regime's current wishes. While the Department of Cinema in principle has a final say on what can be shown on screen and online, several experts interviewed for this article concur that it is the Central Committee of Inspection, the Central Department of Propaganda and the Ministry of Public Security who are the real censors. This means that censorship is secretive, subtle, sophisticated, subject to interpretation and implemented by a few powerful individuals.

In July 2023, the highly anticipated Barbie movie was banned from domestic distribution in Vietnam because of a scene featuring an ambiguous map that supposedly showed the nine-dash line – the map markings which indicate territory claimed by China in the South China Sea.

Censorship is secretive, subtle, sophisticated, subject to interpretation and implemented by a few powerful individuals

But journalists and Vietnam observers remain clueless as to what exactly the problem was with a random map in the movie.

Similarly, when Quan Kế Huy won the Oscar for Best Supporting Actor in 2022 with the movie Everything Everywhere All at Once, domestic media outlets initially pulsated with celebratory messages about how he was the first actor of Vietnamese origin to scoop an Oscar. The actor's speech about being a boat person who ended up in a refugee camp but was now on "Hollywood's biggest stage" was also picked up.

But the mood soon cooled.

There were heated debates on social media, where most Vietnamese people turn for updates on political events at home and abroad, about whether it was appropriate to celebrate him. According to Hằng, a state-affiliated journalist who didn't want to be named, her editor warned her and her young colleagues to be careful when mentioning Quan. The Central Department of Propaganda, which decides what the 800 media outlets in the country can publish, had issued an ambiguous rule to limit coverage of his Oscar win.

"It was then safer to just mention he is of Asian heritage," said Hằng, who explained that the penalty for journalists who broke unwritten rules was severe. "It is [now] best not to write about him anymore."

The millions of boat people who fled the Chinese and Vietnamese communist regimes in the wake of the fall of Saigon in 1975 (known in Vietnam as The Reunification) remains a taboo topic inside Vietnam, as are the many who were killed at sea as they fled. The highly censored textbooks and muzzled media meant young journalists were at first not aware that talking about Quan might cause trouble.

Young people know only that the communist army liberated Southern Vietnam from the shackles of the American invaders and their Southern Vietnamese puppet regime. They barely know that there were two Vietnams between 1955 and 1975, or that the triumph of the communists was synonymous with the tragic demise of the fledgling Republic of Vietnam.

Quan's history is even more complicated. The Vietnamese exodus in the 1970s was far from homogeneous. Quan is Vietnamese but ethnically Chinese. He fled in 1978 during the split between two communist comrades-cum-brothers (China and Vietnam) which led to the expulsion of ethnic Chinese people who lived in Vietnam.

In 1979, there was a brief but bloody border war between Vietnam and China – the first war between two communist countries. Numerous border skirmishes continued until 1990 when the two normalised ties, but only on condition that no one spoke about the past.

"There are more foreign movies than reported in the media," said Ngọc who works for a film marketing company, but didn't want their real name to be used.

For example, the 2023 South Korean movie Our Season was not allowed to be screened in Vietnam despite its non-political content. The reason for the ban was its main actress, Shin Min-a, who once featured in a 10-minute music video titled Do You Know? The music video is accused of insulting the Vietnamese army and distorting Vietnamese history because it shows South Korean soldiers protecting Vietnamese people from Vietnamese forces. In fact, telling a narrative in any form of media diverging from the CPV-approved history is a criminal offence.

A Hanoi-based university lecturer on cinema who also did not want to be named told Index: "When it comes to sexual content or explicit violence or violations of territorial sovereignty, reasons are explicitly stated and published on state-affiliated media."

Yet when a ban on a movie is because of alternative narratives on war, it is less publicised or denounced, with very vague statements, as being a distortion of history.

In 2021, the streaming giant Netflix, which is now seeking to open an office in the fast-growing and digitally dynamic Vietnam, was forced to withdraw six episodes of its spy drama Pine Gap after regulators found it contained "illegal images" of the nine-dash line.

The lecturer was not surprised as "every movie, overseas or homegrown, goes through censorship, from →

RIGHT: Quan Kế Huy at the Vanity Fair Oscar Party in Los Angeles

→ scriptwriting to release".

Little Women, a Korean series adapted from the classic novel of the same name, was also removed from Netflix Vietnam after being accused by the Vietnamese government of falsifying the history of the Vietnam War in episodes three and eight.

The CPV is far from monolithic. It has always been divided, albeit always looking united. Censorship of movies or cultural products is based on vast and vague rules and the arbitrary and changeable decisions of concerned leaders of various state agencies.

André Menras is an 80-year-old independent filmmaker from France, and the first foreigner to be granted honorary citizenship of Vietnam.

He experienced censorship of his first movie, Hoàng Sa Vietnam: La Meurtrissure (Painful Loss), Hoàng Sa being the Vietnamese name of the Paracel Islands which are contested by Vietnam and China.

In 2011, the year when he was officially granted citizenship, Menras obtained permission to produce the film "as a journalistic product" in Ho Chi Minh City. The film highlighted multiple challenges faced by Vietnamese fishermen in the islands because of regular aggression by Chinese military vessels.

"As soon as [the movie] was released, the film, although viewed and approved by the censors, sparked discontent within the Party," Menras told Index.

He said his film was accused of not "having Party characteristics" and lacking "the Party spirit", meaning that it did not highlight the contribution of the CPV.

For four years, it was banned in Vietnam. It wasn't until 2014 when the Chinese moved their oil drilling platform HD981 closer to the Paracel Islands in what became known as the Hai Yang Shi You 981 standoff, that the film was finally authorised to be publicly shown

ABOVE: Vietnamese fisherman Bui Tan Doan's boat has its cabin door broken off after he says the boat was assaulted with water cannon by a Chinese ship in waters near the Paracel Islands in the South China Sea

in Hanoi, Da Nang and Ho Chi Minh city "simply because it aligned with the party's current objectives".

However, the greenlighting period didn't last long. As Menras remarked: "It has not been screened since then because the submissive relations with Beijing have been restored."

But he has found a simple yet sustainable solution to the ban and has uploaded all his films to YouTube so people can avoid censorship and watch them for free. His fourth short movie, currently in production, will also be shown on the channel.

He refuses to let it dampen his motivation to shed more truths on vulnerable people in his adopted country. ✖

Thiện Việt *is a freelance reporter from Vietnam*

 The two normalised ties, but only on condition that no one spoke about the past

53(03):26/28|DOI:10.1177/03064220241285686

CREDIT: Newscom/Alamy

Fog of war masks descent into authoritarianism

As fears of a regional escalation in the Middle East rise, **BEN LYNFIELD** reports on how Israel is looking increasingly like an authoritarian state

AMID A CRACKDOWN on freedom of expression, Israeli security agencies are saying that a law used to ban Qatari broadcaster Al Jazeera can be deployed to close other foreign outlets. And there are concerns the same law could be easily amended to shut down critical outlets in the Israeli media as well.

"We are not speaking only of al-Jazeera. We will weigh steps against any channel that constitutes an immediate threat to state security," a Shin Bet (Israel's internal security service) official who identified himself only as Eitay told the Knesset's National Security Commitee last month during a hearing I attended extending the Al Jazeera ban.

It was first banned in May on the grounds the station, which Israel claims backs Hamas but also subverts Israeli domination of the flow of war information, was substantively harming state security and inciting violence against Israelis. The station denies this.

Eitay's declaration was just one example of how the Israeli security apparatus – including the Shin Bet and the police under the control of far-right national security minister Itamar Ben-Gvir – is flexing its muscles and expanding its clout while the public and media are preoccupied with the seemingly unwinnable war against Hamas in Gaza.

At the Knesset, the committee room was eventually partially cleared so that Eitay could present classified material, a practice typical of the secretive process by which the ban on Al Jazeera, with its significant ramifications, has coasted through the power structure.

Spy agency Mossad, for its part, was hardly a restraining actor. "Mossad also supports the necessity of limiting foreign channels, of course with each case being examined on its merits," its official said during the open part of the hearing. A military censor chimed in with his approval, too.

Zvika Fogel, a retired brigadier general from Ben-Gvir's Otzma Yehudit party, who last year praised the torching by extremist settlers of a Palestinian town in the occupied West Bank, chaired the meeting with enthusiasm.

"From what [information] I am exposed to, foreign journalists are harming the security of the state," he said, suggesting that Israel's enemies were getting information from foreign journalists enabling them to hit targets in northern Israel from Lebanon. He offered no proof, nor was he asked to do so.

Al Jazeera was an easy first target among the media because it is widely viewed in Israel as an enemy mouthpiece. But the precedent has been set and, as the hearings demonstrate, it will now be more straightforward to close other outlets. The security agency recommendations enabling the government to close foreign outlets are supposed to be subject to judicial review – but only after they have already been shuttered.

Given a tradition in which judges seldom challenge the Shin Bet, and the fact that the recommendations are based at least partly on secret evidence which the appellant cannot even access, Israel lacks adequate safeguards to protect foreign media outlets.

The Association for Civil Rights in Israel is mounting a last-ditch effort to strike down the original foreign outlets closure law at the supreme court. But it is a long shot after earlier judicial rounds failed to dent the ever-expanding ideology of state security.

"This is a slippery slope. Now it's Al Jazeera, then it could be another foreign station, maybe Sky News in Arabic or CNN, and then Channel 12," Oren Persico, a staffer at the Seventh ➔

ABOVE: Protesters hold a banner in support of press freedom in Israel outside the Blavatnik Building at Tate Modern in London. UK billionaire Len Blavatnik's Access Entertainment company owns more than 50% of Channel 13

 The less the public knows, the more disciplined it will be

ABOVE: Israeli Minister of National Security, Itamar Ben Gvir at the Damascus Gate in Jerusalem surrounded by Israelis, many of them ultra-nationalists, who are taking part in the Jerusalem Day flag march through the Muslim Quarter in what is considered an act of provocation to Palestinians

→ Eye media watchdog, said. Channel 12 is Israel's most popular outlet, featuring both critics and supporters of the coalition.

The pressure in Israel, a country which was once considered a relatively bright spot in the repressive Middle Eastern media environment, is not just being exercised by security figures. Liberal Israeli journalists shifted into survival mode last month after a major television outlet, Channel 13, appointed as their new news editor Yulia Shamalov-Berkovich, a former legislator, perceived as a supporter of prime minister Benjamin Netanyahu.

While many journalists from the channel and their supporters have poor credentials as champions of free expression because of their glaring failure to report the massive suffering and death among civilians in Gaza during the war, the station nevertheless still broadcasts investigations into government misconduct and is generally considered independent.

After Shamalov-Berkovich's appointment changes came quickly. War Zone, a show fronted by investigative journalist Raviv Drucker with a history of challenging Netanyahu, was canned.

This decision intensified journalists' fears of Channel 13, owned by UK billionaire Len Blavatnik, becoming simply a pro-Netanyahu outlet, especially as Drucker had recently carried out a damning probe into alleged corruption in the transport ministry.

This is a slippery slope. Now it's Al Jazeera, then it could be another foreign station

CREDIT: Eyal Warshavsky/Alamy

It was all in line with what Israel Journalist Association media freedom officer Anat Saragusti terms a "master plan" for destroying independent media.

Channel 13 employees reacted by calling an emergency protest in July, which was also attended by journalists from other outlets and they mounted a legal challenge to Shamalov-Berkovich's appointment. The following month the management agreed to an out-of-court agreement to reverse it.

But Saragusti warned that journalists must remain vigilant. Other components of the government's media plans,

Saragusti says, include following up on communications minister Shlomo Karhi's threats to cripple the Kan public broadcasting corporation, an Israeli version of the BBC with diverse voices, and to strengthen Channel 14, an unabashedly pro-Netanyahu channel that targets coalition critics.

She said the coalition government's approach to the media was motivated by the same anti-democratic goals as its efforts to weaken the judiciary, a measure that kicked off mass protests last year.

"They want to eliminate gatekeepers, whether in the judiciary or in a free media, whose job is to criticise the government and shed light in dark places," she said. "The less the public knows, the more disciplined it will be, and the less it will demonstrate and rise up when it is harmed."

The security rationale, which resonates in a country where the security establishment has always played a huge role – including by imposing what amounts to a military dictatorship on Palestinians – is being invoked in other areas too.

After the 7 October Hamas incursion into Israel, the massacre of more than 1000 Israelis, the taking of hostages, and the war in which Israeli soldiers have killed more than 40,000 Palestinians, freedom of expression is being limited on social media, demonstrations are being suppressed and academic freedom curtailed. The coalition is projecting the message that survival is at stake and there needs to be heightened vigilance against threats.

"7 October just strengthened our belief that all our enemies are coming to destroy us," Likud legislator Eliyahu Revivo told me in May.

He was explaining why he was advancing an amendment to a 2016 anti-terrorism law that would broaden the definition of punishable incitement. The old version of the law has already been widely used against Palestinian citizens of Israel who write social media posts with messages ranging from support for the Hamas attacks to expressions of sympathy for Palestinians under Israeli bombardment in Gaza.

"This amendment will give more flexibility to the police to arrest and indict," says Hassan Jabareen, director of Adalah, a legal advocacy group for Israel's Arab minority.

He said a chilling effect has spread, and police were violating the rights of Arabs and a small number of far-left Jews to protest.

"This war is totally different from the other wars because the police themselves are really working against the law," he said. "They arrest people for no reason and prohibit protests by force even when the protest doesn't require a licence."

The chill is also pronounced in academia, according to Jabareen. He said: "I get phone calls from professors wondering whether their syllabus will be a problem or not." On 11 July the Knesset approved on preliminary reading a bill that would require university heads to fire, without severance pay, instructors who are deemed to support terrorism. In the event of non-compliance, the institution's budget could be cut.

Ksenia Svetlova, a political analyst who was a journalist and a left-wing opposition member of the Knesset, is deeply troubled. She believes the war is accelerating a process by which the coalition is transforming Israel not into an illiberal democracy, as feared last year, but into an authoritarian state like Russia. ✖

Ben Lynfield is a freelance journalist based in Jerusalem

53(03):29/31|DOI:10.1177/03064220241285687

Movement for the missing

Baloch women and children are more likely to face a water cannon than receive answers when they speak up for missing men in Pakistan, writes **ANMOL IRFAN**

N EARLY MARCH, Baloch student Khudadad Siraj disappeared from the University of Sargodha in Punjab, leading to protests across campus that were quickly shut down by security forces.

Siraj allegedly had not just disappeared but was the victim of an "enforced disappearance" – a term used to describe the state authorities suddenly taking someone into custody and effectively making them disappear.

Siraj is not the only one to have faced this.

Baloch communities have been living in fear of enforced disappearances for generations, with little respite or support from outside parties.

Voice for Missing Baloch Persons, an organisation representing the families of people who have gone missing in Balochistan – a province of Pakistan – say the number of people who have been "disappeared" since 2013 stands at 8,000, and community activists say that hundreds, if not thousands, were victims before then.

Siraj's disappearance comes on the heels of the Baloch Long March, a historic women-led march and sit-in, where around 400 Baloch protesters – half of them women and children – marched from Turbat to Islamabad last winter following the killing of 24-year-old Balaach Mola Baksh. But instead of being met with answers, the protesters

ABOVE: Members of the Baloch Students Council Punjab protest against the enforced disappearance of students

CREDIT: Pakistan Press International (PPI) / Alamy

being involved in terrorist activities.

His family, who were part of the march, are staunchly claiming otherwise, saying he had nothing to do with any of these activities and was falsely accused.

It was Baksh's death that incited the march, but the movement to bring back loved ones who have been forcibly disappeared is far older. It is a struggle that has shaped the lives of generations of Baloch men who live in fear every day, and women and children who spend their lives worrying not only about their loved ones but also about supporting themselves and having to carry on, not knowing if their family members are dead or alive.

"This is not the first time that Baloch women have come to the forefront to struggle for the safe release of their loved ones," said Sammi Deen Baloch, a human rights activist and one of the leading faces in the movement against enforced disappearances.

"Since 2001, the Baloch mothers have been on the roads and demanding justice."

Each time, the women are pushed back – both physically, as in the case of the Long March, and in the media, through a nationwide silencing of Baloch issues. Just days after Index spoke to Sammi Deen Baloch, reports emerged that she had been arrested.

"The state of Pakistan has left us with no options except protesting and struggling for the safe release of our loved ones," she said. "This Long March has made the Baloch women a symbol of resistance and demonstrated to the world that Baloch women are courageous, are resolute and can fight for the lives of their men."

Her father, Deen Muhammad Baloch, has been missing since 2009 and his daughter has no idea if he is even still alive.

The Long March has been covered extensively on social media and internationally, highlighting the struggles

and resilience of leaders such as doctor Mahrang Baloch.

It is a resilience she has developed through marching since she was 10 years old, after her father was forcibly disappeared in 2006. His body was found years later.

"The media enforces a state narrative that no one is missing, and if they are it is because they are terrorists, so the missing person's family's struggle never advances," she said.

Her scepticism despite the enormous effort she puts into fighting for this issue every day is a reminder of the losses she's had to bear throughout this journey.

"Even peaceful movements are ignored, and some journalists even try to paint these peaceful movements as violent," she added.

For many Baloch women and girls, the loss of their fathers, husbands, brothers and sons changes their lives beyond recognition.

"Balochistan is not a very modern place, and so it's not common that a woman can easily lead a movement," lawyer Sadia Baloch told Index. "It is a result of that repression that has forced women to come out and lead, because they have no option and nothing to lose so they are taking on the baton charges and violence."

She explained that she initially got involved with student rights campaigns, adding: "But then you can't stop at that when you see every second day a student just goes 'missing'. They 'disappear' and no one knows what they've done. There are no courts for [them]."

Mahrang and Sadia both note that the fear of not knowing who will be picked up next is one that haunts men, women and children alike.

"There is no one living a normal life. There is insecurity amidst the whole population," said Mahrang. "It's such an intensified issue, there are protests on Eid as well – and even those not affected are always insecure and their mental health declines."

Recent disappearances such as →

– some of whom were as old as 80 – were met with water cannons, batons and arrests when they got to Islamabad.

Baksh's family says that he was picked up from his home while he was sleeping and arrested under alleged terror charges. A day before his intended bail plea hearing on 24 November, Baksh was killed in an encounter in custody after the Counter-Terrorism Department claimed he had confessed to

Baloch women are courageous, are resolute and can fight for the lives of their men

The media enforces a state narrative that no one is missing and if they are it is because they are terrorists

→ Siraj's have quickly taught Baloch families that their sons and brothers are not safe even in other parts of the country. Yet those losses and efforts such as the Long March are not highlighted in the media as much as acts of militancy in the province, painting a skewed picture of what Baloch people actually want.

"Peaceful protests have never been given importance in the country of Pakistan and that is the reason why the concept of violence is increasing day by day instead of peaceful struggle," said Sammi, adding: "I have always believed in peaceful struggle and I have been peacefully protesting against forced disappearances for the past 15 years."

For young children who have visited jails more times than they have been to school, violence has played a key role in shaping their lives. They are innocent citizens caught up between two sides, and because they're an easy target, they become the victims.

Sadia explained that individuals can feel as though they're not making an impact. But she said they can make a difference.

"If there's a child whose father is missing, sponsor their education as there's usually one [bread winner] so their leaving creates a financial crisis for many families."

It is individual efforts such as these that show there is some hope that the new generation of Baloch youth might be able to escape the violence they see every day, and through allyship be able to demand change. ✖

Anmol Irfan is a journalist based in Pakistan

53(03):32/34|DOI:10.1177/03064220241285689

Mob, jury and executioner

Lynchings after allegations of blasphemy have become commonplace in Pakistan, writes ZOFEEN T EBRAHIM

THE MOB LYNCHING of Mohammad Salman in June, followed by the burning of his body, has shaken residents from the idyllic Swat Valley in Khyber Pakhtunkhwa, Karachi. According to media reports, Salman was from Malaysia and was visiting family when he was accused of burning pages from the Quran.

"This is a stain our town will carry forever," said 52-year-old Ehsanuddin (who goes by one name), a local baker who talked to Index over the phone from Madyan, where it happened.

Ehsanuddin saw the event from his house, "atop the bazaar".

He said he first heard about Salman being in police custody shortly after sunset prayers at the main mosque.

"The crowd kept swelling and went straight towards the police station, where they broke down the gate and torched some vans and started vandalising the station," he said. "It was dark, but because of the fire, I could see everything. The incensed crowd chanting 'Allahu-Akbar, Allahu-Akbar [God is great],' went around in search of the man. The policemen who tried to ward them off were beaten by the angry mob.

"The man was found and was dragged – all the while [they were] hitting him – up to the bazaar. I am not sure if he had died of his injuries or was still alive when they burnt the lifeless body."

Much of this was corroborated by a senior investigating officer, who requested that his name be withheld.

"Some 2,5000 people have been officially charged for this event and 42 arrested so far," he said.

Under the law, defiling or insulting the prophet of Islam, his companions or family members, or desecrating the Quran is an offence for which the penalty is death or life imprisonment.

"At least 100 persons have been killed extra-judicially over blasphemy allegations since 1994," said Peter Jacob, executive director of the Pakistan-based research and policy advocacy organisation Centre for Social Justice, which has been keeping a close watch on the numbers.

On 25 May, Nazir Gill Masih, an elderly Christian shoemaker, was attacked by a mob in Sargodha, a city in Punjab province, after a local cleric accused him of blasphemy.

His factory and home were set ablaze, and he died in hospital on 3 June. Islamist extremist political party Tehreek-e-Labbaik Pakistan (TLP) protested the arrest of those accused of killing him.

Last August, thousands of people set churches and Christians' homes on fire in Jaranwala, also in Punjab, because of allegations of desecration of the Quran.

Al Jazeera found the party flag of the TLP lying near the altar of one of the 22 destroyed churches, but the party has denied any involvement.

In 2021, a Sri Lankan factory manager was killed by a mob in Sialkot after untrue rumours spread of a blasphemous action.

Maulana Muhammad Tayyab Qureshi, the chief *khateeb* (prayer leader) of the Khyber Pakhtunkhwa province and a member of the National Commission for Human Rights Pakistan, a state institution, told Index that it was sad to see innocent people killed by mobs over allegations of blasphemy.

"What is needed is proper training of our law enforcement agencies to pre-empt such events and act swiftly to diffuse the situation," he said.

"Even if proof is found, can a mob become the judge, jury and executioner? Why [do we] have the courts and the judges, then?"

Zofeen T Ebrahim is a freelance journalist based in Karachi, Pakistan

Mental manipulation

Vladimir Putin is using psychiatrists as a weapon to silence dissidents, writes **ALEXANDRA DOMENECH**

"THERE IS NO bigger crime than the killing of the soul. Stop punitive psychiatry!" read the sign held by activist Oksana Osadchaya at a solo protest in the centre of Moscow in June.

The activist – who is visually impaired – was making her protest even though the tiniest acts of dissent can lead to severe punishment.

She was taken to a police station where she wasn't allowed to meet her lawyer at first, and was released without charge only after being held for several hours.

Osadchaya's desperate act of protest was meant to draw attention to the use of enforced psychiatric treatment in Russia against defendants in politically motivated cases.

According to independent media outlet Agentstvo, at least 33 such cases have been documented since 2023, when people arrested for opposing the war in Ukraine started being sentenced. Between 2013 and 2022 there were just 22.

A new bill, which will become law in 2025, will allow the police to gain access to the medical records of people

ABOVE: Police escort Viktoria Petrova to a hearing in St Petersburg in March 2023

suffering from certain mental illnesses and who are deemed by psychiatrists to be a threat to public order.

Dmitry Kutovoy, a member of Russia's Psychiatric Association, told Index he had concerns that amending legislation could contribute to creating a system of oppression using psychiatry. He warned that the authorities might put pressure on medical workers to →

A person is arrested holding a sign, taken to a police station, and a psychiatric team is called

→ designate certain people as "activists, political opponents, and so on".

One recent high-profile case was that of Viktoria Petrova, who was arrested in May 2022. She was accused of "spreading false information" about the Russian military in anti-war social media posts.

Activist Anush Panina went to support Petrova during her trial in St Petersburg.

"All of a sudden, the court announced that the hearings would be closed to the public, and sent her to a psychiatric hospital," Panina remembered, speaking to Index from exile.

"It was outrageous and frightening."

Panina suspects Petrova was punished for continuing to speak up while in detention and on trial. In her final statement to the court, Petrova said that Russia's war in Ukraine was "a crime against humanity".

Panina felt it was "convenient" for the authorities to put an end to the public trial on grounds of medical confidentiality and said that, at previous hearings, bogus experts who had analysed Petrova's social media posts had proved to be so incompetent that people were laughing at them.

At the psychiatric unit, Petrova was brutalised by the medical staff, according to her lawyer Anastasia Pilipenko.

She was forced to undress while male nurses were watching, and after she refused to take a shower in front of them, they twisted her arms and threatened to beat her. She was tied to a bed and injected with heavy medications which left her barely able to speak for two days.

Adding that it was unclear whether the abuse had been ordered by the Kremlin, Panina said Petrova's treatment course could be extended indefinitely, and a medical commission would convene every six months to decide whether to prolong it. In August, soon after Panina spoke with Index, Petrova was released from the psychiatric unit. She will now be observed on an outpatient basis.

Kutovoy said that cases of inhumane treatment such as Petrova's were, at least for the moment, "isolated incidents". He added, however, that enforced psychiatric treatment in Russia today was nevertheless "as scary as it sounds".

"Patients' rights aren't really respected," he explained, adding that heavy medications were given to them at high dosages.

Kutovoy said that, in theory, enforced treatment was ordered by the court instead of punishment. "In practice, however, it's still punishment – just in a different form," he said.

But considering the long prison sentences handed out to dissidents under President Vladimir Putin, enforced treatment may be the lesser evil in certain circumstances. This seems to be the case with Viktor Moskalev, another defendant in an anti-war criminal case who was sent to a psychiatric ward.

In March 2023, he was arrested for "spreading false information" about the Russian army after making two comments about war crimes committed in Ukraine on the e-xecutive.ru website.

Moskalev's lawyer, Mikhail Biryukov, told Index that in 2005, his client had been diagnosed with a mental illness in a private clinic. He was now in remission, and "has a prospect of being set free [from the psychiatric unit] earlier than if he were in prison".

Abuse of psychiatry to persecute and intimidate state critics was a popular practice in the Soviet Union. Dissident Alexander Skobov was condemned to compulsory psychiatric treatment twice, in the 1970s and the 1980s.

In May this year, he was sent to a psychiatric unit again, for "examination". He is accused of posting messages justifying terrorism on social media, as well as of taking part in a terrorist organisation, and could face up to 22 years in jail.

"The repressive machine is looking for new methods of persecution," Kutovoy said. "It's just the way it works."

According to Kutovoy, this trend points towards a punitive mechanism of using psychiatry being in demand by the authorities. He said there had been an increase in the number of involuntary hospitalisations of arrested political protesters.

"A person is arrested holding a sign, is taken to a police station, and a psychiatric team is called," he explained. "Then the psychiatrists have to decide whether there is a need for involuntary hospitalisation."

If they conclude that's the case – and, a few days later, decide that this measure must be maintained – the court can order long-term compulsory treatment.

Kutovoy emphasised that in many cases, psychiatrists refused to send dissidents to hospital against their will. Alexey Sokirko, for example, was arrested in July for wearing a T-shirt which read: "I'm against Putin". Police officers called a psychiatric team after Sokirko asked them whether an "I'm against Stalin" tag would be allowed. In the end, the doctors concluded that there was no need for involuntary hospitalisation.

Kutovoy said he wished he could speak out more openly on the issue of punitive psychiatry. However, he added: "In Russia today, it's impossible to make a statement which is not in line with the political agenda [of the state]. And there is an obvious connection between cases of abuse of psychiatric care and the political agenda." ✖

Alexandra Domenech is a Moscow-born, Paris-based journalist specialising in women's rights in Russia

53(03):35/36|DOI:10.1177/03064220241285698

The fight for India's media freedom

Index has been working closely with an extraordinary group of independent Indian journalists appointed as visiting media fellows at the University of Essex. The three articles we publish here demonstrate the challenging landscape in which they are working and the vital role they play as Prime Minister Narendra Modi continues to demand unquestioning loyalty from the mainstream media in India

53(03):37/39| 10.1177/03064220241285699

Money's too tight to mention

ANGANA CHAKRABARTI reports from the North Eastern region, where government advertising is used as a tool to control the media

THE FOUR EDITORS of Assam's English daily, The Drongo Express, meet in person once or twice a month. They sit hunched over their laptops and notebooks – either at parks or in someone's house in Diphu, where the paper is headquartered – figuring out how to keep their newspaper afloat.

One of them, Helvellyn Timungpi, from the tribal district of Karbi Anglong, told Index: "Last year, our publisher decided to walk away from the newspaper. We who were on the editorial board came together and signed the partnership deed and got a transfer of ownership. We didn't have any other employment, and we wanted to stop this newspaper from going down the drain."

Like many newspapers in North East India – which is made up of eight states including Assam – The Drongo Express relies heavily on advertisements placed by government departments. "We haven't received a single penny since last October," said Timungpi. "If we were receiving our bills regularly, we would be OK."

Home to about 140 notified Scheduled Tribes [indigenous groups], the region remains poorly covered by the mainstream media. Most Delhi-based media houses continue to employ just one reporter in the region. Others send journalists to cover only stories of extreme violence – for instance, the ongoing ethnic conflict in Manipur or the botched security operation in Nagaland that led to several civilian deaths. Local news channels, newspapers and websites have played a significant role in filling this gap.

Karma Paljor, a former news anchor and founder of EastMojo – the first and only independent digital news outlet that primarily covers the North East – said media ownership was a big problem.

"Anyone with a reasonable amount of money, including contractors, lobbyists and politicians can start a media organisation," he said. "There are very few newspapers here that stand for balanced news."

The demographic complexity of the region also plays a part.

"On account of the region's layered contemporary history as well as ethnic and linguistic faultlines, most local publications do tend to be nativist and, in many cases, unabashedly take sides on polarising topics such as immigration," explained Tora Agarwala, an independent journalist based in Assam.

Media organisations in the region are often faced with a lack of revenue and resources. Kenter Joya, the managing editor of the Arunachal Pradesh-based Eastern Sentinel, said: "The cost of printing papers is 15 rupees, and we are selling it at three rupees. Vendors take 50% of this money ... we try to make it up through advertisements from state government, which constitute 65% of advertisements placed, and corporate advertisements.

"Annually, bi-annually, we receive only 50-60% of what we are owed for the advertisements."

She said she wondered if payment was being withheld as a form of punishment.

Meanwhile, repeated calls for subscriptions, especially by independent outlets such as EastMojo, haven't yielded many results.

"The people of the North East are not aware of the power of media, hence they aren't able to fathom why they should support us," Paljor said.

"I don't know who to blame," said an exasperated Timungpi. "No matter how penniless I become, I want to cling to this profession. But it pains me when my three children have nothing to eat."

Angana Chakrabarti is an independent journalist in the North Eastern region of India

> Contractors, lobbyists and politicians can start a media organisation. There are very few newspapers here that stand for balanced news

CREDIT: Handout

Living in gangster times

Reporting on organised crime in the eastern state of Bihar is a deadly business, writes AMIR ABBAS

ON 25 JUNE this year 40-year-old journalist Shivshankar Jha was returning to his home in Muzaffarpur, in the eastern frontier state of Bihar, when he was set upon by a group of men. He was taken to hospital with multiple stab wounds and later died of his injuries.

He worked for several Hindi news outlets in the region and had been reporting on liquor smuggling. His family said he had received death threats and blamed the criminal gangs he had been investigating.

In July, Unesco director-general Audrey Azoulay said: "I condemn the killing of Shivshankar Jha and call for a thorough investigation to ensure that the perpetrators are brought to justice. Journalists play a vital role in investigating crime and wrongdoing, and impunity for crimes against them must not prevail."

This is not an isolated case. Waheed Azam, of Patna-based Democratic Charkha, explained that the illicit trade in alcohol and raw materials such as sand was open to exploitation from criminal gangs.

"Journalism in Bihar is extremely challenging," he said. "The last decade has been marked by political instability, with frequent changes in government. Meanwhile, illegal liquor smuggling and the sand mafia have shaken the state's economy. If you publish a report that displeases the mafia or those in power, you end up either dead or framed in false cases."

Madhubani is globally renowned for its ancient tradition of painting. However, on 12 November 2021, the headlines were not about the city's art but about the brutal murder of a 26-year-old journalist named Avinash Jha.

Jha, who worked for the local news website BNN, was found dead, his body charred beyond recognition. He had been missing for three days.

He had published a series of news reports exposing illegal nursing homes operating in the district, after which he began receiving threatening phone calls. His last Facebook post read: "A major exposé on illegal nursing homes is coming soon."

Kanhaiya Mishra, the editor of BNN News

in Madhubani, called on the Central Bureau of Investigation to take up his colleague's case.

"There was never an impartial investigation. Initially, the police tried to frame the murder as the result of a love affair, but everyone knows why Avinash [Jha] was killed," he said.

One of the most notorious cases was the 2016 murder of Rajdev Ranjan in Siwan.

Ranjan, 46, had recently become bureau chief at the Hindustan Daily, where he had published several reports on the criminal

> Everyone knows who ordered his murder, but people are too scared to even mention his name. Why? Because he is a powerful gangster and a former MP

activities of former MP and notorious gangster Mohammad Shahabuddin. His final report focused on how Shahabuddin continued to operate his gang from behind bars.

The Bihar police and the CBI have a track record of failure in solving journalists' murders. In the Ranjan case, the CBI told a court in 2022 that the key witness, Badami Devi, had died.

She later appeared in court with all her identification documents.

Ranjan's wife, Asha Devi, recalled: "The day after his murder was supposed to be our wedding anniversary. I was waiting for him, but he never came back. Everyone knows who ordered his murder, but people are too scared to even mention his name. Why? Because he is a powerful gangster and a former MP."

Two common threads run through these cases: all the journalists were local reporters, covering grassroots issues in Bihar, and none of the cases has resulted in the conviction of the perpetrators. Bihar ranks high for incidents of violence against journalists but, living in the poorest and most backward state in the country, its local journalists often find no one to take up their cause.

Amir Abbas runs a team of hyper-local journalists who write about Bihar issues

ABOVE: Journalists hold a protest against the murder of a journalist in the Siwan district of Bihar in Allahabad in 2016.

The show must go on

RAVISH KUMAR was one of the biggest independent voices of Indian channel NDTV before he dramatically resigned to set up his own YouTube channel in 2022. Vrinda Sharma has been at his side ever since

WE KNEW IT was coming. It was 28 November 2021, and I was meeting my friend Ravish for the first time in nearly 20 months.

Because of Covid I had been working from home since March 2020; a home that was 660km away from Delhi.

It was a smoggy winter, as is usually the case in Delhi, but that day was a bright sunny one. We walked along Lodhi Road, and at one point in our conversation Ravish turned to me and said with a grim smile: "Don't worry. When NDTV shuts down, we will set up a YouTube channel."

Such comments were not new for him, but this was the first time Ravish had spoken of what would happen after our jobs had gone.

I would always brush away such fearful forecasts, and I disregarded this one until August 2022, when NDTV was taken over by billionaire Gautam Adani.

In November of that year – almost exactly a year after that winter afternoon on Lodhi Road, as the takeover neared completion – Ravish quit. The YouTube channel that we run today – Ravish Kumar Official – became operational with the release of his resignation episode.

The response at the time was overwhelming. In the first month, more than 2.75 million people subscribed to the channel. Ravish and I never formally sat down to discuss working together. I was far more clueless than I had ever been but also sure of the fact that, for a variety of reasons, I was part of something momentous. And I knew I wanted to be here.

My first experience of the editorial independence we had bought for ourselves came two months after we started.

In January 2023, US financial forensic investigators Hindenburg Research issued a critical report on Adani's companies, which led to a collapse in stock prices.

Throughout the next few days, we regularly reported on the story on our channel, and realised that we were on different turf now. We did not have the

ABOVE: A still from the documentary While We Watched about Ravish Kumar's struggles to tell the truth at NDTV. Two months after it was made, Kumar resigned to set up his own YouTube channel

resources of a TV station. We had no network of journalists to rely on. We could not afford lights and live transmission systems. We struggled with visuals as everything was copyrighted. We were a small team of four yet, somehow, we managed.

It has been 20 months since Ravish's resignation. In that time, I have found greater confidence in myself as a journalist. My political sense has evolved and my writing has improved. I can produce and edit very quickly and can create compelling reports on the most meagre of resources.

I have started my own series called Vox

We did not have the resources of a TV station. We had no network of journalists to rely on

Vrinda, but it has not been an easy ride. After five years of working under the regime in India, I now know that censorship works in insidious ways.

It is not just about the jailing of a journalist. It is also about making their life and livelihood so precarious that they question their choices every waking moment.

Every other day, Ravish and I talk about what will happen when this channel is taken down. As a young female journalist, I do not know what my future looks like in this profession. The powers that govern my life and want to control my voice have received electoral shocks, but they are as vicious as ever.

It is true that my experience as a journalist is informed by the very stifling political environment that I am in – but it has also been about finding my way and my voice by knocking my knees and elbows against all that comes my way.

I know the path ahead is not an easy walk, but I have good shoes on.

VRINDA SHARMA *is a journalist for Ravish Kumar Official and presenter of Vox Vrinda*

A black, green and red flag to repression

Photojournalist **MEHRAN FIRDOUS** reports on a crackdown on pro-Palestine sentiment at a procession in Kashmir

KASHMIR'S ANNUAL MUHARRAM observances, which began on 8 July, have taken on a new dimension, after the procession for the eighth day was banned in Srinagar from 1989 until last year. While traditionally marked by mourning for Imam Hussain – the Prophet Mohammed's grandson – the Shia community used the 2024 gatherings as a platform to express solidarity with the Palestinian people through large-scale demonstrations where flags and symbols were carried in a poignant display of support.

The conflict between India and Pakistan over Kashmir has fuelled decades of violence, with a marked increase in suppression of dissent after the 2019 revocation of the region's semi-autonomous status. The pro-Palestinian marches resonate with Kashmiri protesters, who find parallels with their own struggle.

But the authorities' response has been severe, leading to the detention and questioning of many Shia mourners, and raising freedom of expression concerns.

Authorities in Kashmir filed an open case at Kothi Bagh police station under new criminal codes against mourners for allegedly raising pro-Palestine and pro-Hezbollah placards and flags.

Aga Syed Ruhullah Mehdi, a member of the Indian parliament from Kashmir, posted on X that the police had arrested several youths "for raising slogans in favour of the people of Palestine and carrying [the] Palestine flag". He condemned the arrests as an assault on freedom of expression. ✖

53(03):40/43|DOI:10.1177/03064220241285700

PICTURED: Kashmiri Shia mourners raise placards in support of Palestine during a *Muharram* rally in the interior of Dal Lake in Srinagar

PICTURED: A Shia
mourner watches the
Muharram procession
in the Dalgate area of
Srinagar, with his face
painted in the colours
of the Palestinian flag

PICTURED: Kashmiri Shia Muslims stage a sit-in protest in support of Palestine during a *Muharram* rally in Srinagar.

PICTURED: Thousands of Shia mourners march through the centre of Srinagar city, commemorating the eighth day of *Muharram*, the first month of the Islamic lunar calendar.

PICTURED: A Shia
Muslim girl waves
a Palestinian flag
during a *Muharram*
rally in Srinagar

CREDIT: Mehran Firdous

PICTURED: A Shia
Muslim participant in a
Muharram procession
wears a t-shirt with a
message of solidarity
for Palestine

The inventive new biography of Franz Kafka

'A high-spirited, richly informed and original portrait' Marina Warner

Metamorphoses

In Search of Franz Kafka

Karolina Watroba

'A brilliant young scholar' *Spectator*

Out Now

SPECIAL REPORT

INCONVENIENT TRUTHS

"If the state had nothing to hide regarding what caused Honourable Nebanda's death, why has it blocked Dr Onzivua from flying to Pretoria?"

DEATH AND MINOR DETAILS | DANSON KAHYANA | P60

Choked by ideology

The West shouldn't worry too much about Chinese technological progress, writes **MURONG XUECUN**, because politics is stifling new thought

" I 'VE BEEN TEACHING mathematics for half my life and never thought I'd see something like this," said Mr Liu (who doesn't want us to publish his full name).

Liu is referring to a textbook on advanced mathematics published in China two years ago, which includes a lot of new content that has nothing

to do with mathematics: Karl Marx's discourse on mathematics, and president Xi Jinping's discourse on Marx's discourse on mathematics.

These discourses are part of "ideological and political education".

According to a government document released in 2021, the purpose of adding this content is to "guide students to realise the power of truth of Xi Jinping's thoughts" and "educate and guide students to build up a lofty communist ideal and patriotism".

For people such as Liu, these things didn't make them more patriotic – they were outraged.

"What the heck, it is ridiculous!" said Liu.

In recent years, Liu has been living in Australia, and it is difficult for him to understand the bizarre changes in his homeland. However, for people living in China, such changes are not unusual. Even those who are angry do not say so publicly.

Although this Communist country has always viewed mathematics as being important, the government believes politics – that is, the ideas of the great leader – is even more important.

And it's not just mathematics. In the near future there will be similar content in physics, chemistry, astronomy and all other textbooks.

Perhaps it has already happened. Putting Xi Jinping's name ahead of science also means that for the foreseeable future, science, especially Chinese science, must not go against Xi Jinping Thought, which, let's not forget, has "the power of truth" according to the *gaokao* exams taken by school leavers on the leader's ideology. If there is any conflict between science and this thought – which happens all the time – it must be science that is wrong.

In the 1960s and 1970s, even in the remote mountain villages of China, people all knew Albert Einstein's name – not because they loved his physics – but because Beijing believed that Einstein had made a terrible mistake and they organised critique after critique.

Even in the small village where I was born, the townsfolk, the uneducated peasants and the rural cadres all believed that Einstein was a bourgeois lapdog.

One of my elders once made a public statement at a mass rally. Not knowing the correct pronunciation of Einstein, he mistakenly called him "Aiyastan".

"There is an Aiyastan in America who says that truth is relative. What crap! Chairman Mao's thought is the absolute truth!"

At that time, not only did the Chinese population not study Einstein but all the universities were closed.

History repeats itself, especially in countries such as China. Now, thousands – or possibly millions – of Chinese people, mostly of the younger generations, believe in Western pseudo-history: that Socrates and Plato were fictional and that the Western calendar was borrowed from China.

They say "Western civilisation" does not exist at all, and all the Western discoveries and achievements – including political systems, AI and quantum physics – came from a 15th century Chinese encyclopedia. The West shamelessly stole the fruits of our civilisation and never dared to admit it.

Again, such ideas should not come as a surprise. It is easy to find the source of these bizarre arguments by looking through official Chinese documents, in which Xi repeatedly says that we must strengthen our cultural confidence, and that "Chinese civilisation is the only great civilisation in the world that has continued to this day". All you need to remember is "the only great civilisation".

Xi himself has many unscientific and anti-scientific views, such as his famous remark: "Traditional Chinese medicine [TCM] is the treasure of ancient Chinese science and the key to unlocking the treasury of Chinese civilisation."

In China, Xi's words are more powerful than the law, and it is under the guidance of these words that China has built a large number of new TCM hospitals and institutes in recent years. During the Covid pandemic, these institutions concocted numerous remedies.

One that I saw had six ingredients, including orange peel, mulberry leaf and reed root. They believed this potion could cure Covid infections and distributed it to tens of thousands of patients.

People in the West often talk worriedly about China's scientific and technological progress. They refer to all kinds of data: the number of Chinese patents, the number of Chinese students studying in the West, how many Chinese scientific papers are published, and how often these papers are cited.

The numbers may be accurate, and the scholars' concerns are justified. But this should only be a minor concern. A moment of worry is fine, but it shouldn't last for too long.

Something else is also important – perhaps even more important.

What is the significance and place of science in Chinese life? What do Chinese scientists do? And how many rights and freedoms do they have?

The Law of the People's Republic of China on Scientific and Technological Progress, signed by Xi and promulgated in 2021, is the most important law on scientific research in China.

While it mentions "respect for knowledge" and "respect for talent", there is a more important clause that goes above and beyond everything else: "To adhere to the overall leadership of the Communist Party of China in the cause of science and technology."

This means that science in China not only has borders but also supervisors. There is hardly a single independent scientific institution or university, and every scientist has multiple leaders – administrative, professional, and at least one Communist Party secretary.   →

Putting Xi Jinping's name ahead of science also means that for the foreseeable future, science, especially Chinese science, must not go against Xi Jinping Thought

CREDIT: Badiucao

Hundreds of Uyghur scientists imprisoned in China

Voice of America's KASIM ABDUREHIM KASHGAR says Uyghur science is being censored by the CCP

IF BEING A scientist under Xi Jinping in China is difficult, consider the fate of Uyghur academics and intellectuals.

In recent years, the rights organisation Uyghur Hjelp has documented more than 200 cases of Uyghur scientists and other science professionals being imprisoned in China, according to Abduweli Ayup, founder of the Norway-based group.

Among the most prominent is Tursunjan Nurmamat, who received his graduate and postgraduate education in the United States. Nurmamat, who is from the Xinjiang Uyghur Autonomous Region in northwestern China, specialised in molecular biology and was working as a science editor when he disappeared in 2021.

In addition, he translated English nonfiction books about science and scientists into the Uyghur language. He used his well-known pen name, Bilge, for these translations, which he published on his social media accounts in China.

One of Nurmamat's former employers, Shanghai's Tongji University, confirmed with Radio Free Asia reporters in July 2021 that he had been arrested and had been under investigation since April that year.

In response to a request for more information, Liu Pengyu, spokesperson for the Chinese Embassy in Washington, wrote, "I am not aware of this specific case, thus having nothing to share. China is a law-based country, and I believe the judicial and law enforcement institutions perform their jobs in accordance with law."

Just before Nurmamat's arrest by Xinjiang police, he announced his new role as a science editor at Cell Press, a publisher of scientific journals headquartered in Cambridge, Massachusetts.

"When I last spoke with him before his forced disappearance, he said he was 'stuck and couldn't leave,'" said an exiled Uyghur friend of Nurmamat's now living in Canada [who has asked to remain anonymous]. The Canadian Uyghur, along with several other exiled Uyghurs in the USA who knew Nurmamat before his disappearance, shared details about his situation. They expressed concerns about his well-being in Chinese custody and requested anonymity because of fears for their families in Xinjiang.

Joseph Caputo, head of media and communications at Cell Press, confirmed that Nurmamat had a brief tenure at the organisation but did not provide further details on his current situation.

"No one outside the Chinese government knows his current location or the length of his sentence, similar to many other cases involving Uyghur intellectuals," Uyghur Hjelp's Ayup said.

Uyghur rights organisations say China has been increasing its crackdown on Turkic-speaking Uyghurs in Xinjiang since 2017 with human rights abuses that include arbitrary detention of over one million individuals, forced labour, sterilisation of women and torture.

China's treatment of Uyghurs has been labelled as genocide by the USA and several Western parliaments. The United Nations human rights office has suggested these actions may amount to crimes against humanity.

China denies these accusations, saying Xinjing-related policies are established in the context of combating violent terrorism and separatism, and it accuses the U.S. and Western anti-China forces of spreading disinformation.

Censorship of Uyghur science

Ayup described Nurmamat's case as a key example of the broader censorship affecting Uyghur science and scientists.

"The Chinese government has targeted Uyghur scientists like [Nurmamat] who have studied abroad and experienced democratic freedoms," Ayup said. "His work, including translations and science materials in Uyghur, made him a target."

Ayup noted that by translating and writing extensively in Uyghur about science, Nurmamat directly challenged China's efforts to suppress the Uyghur language in education.

Over the past two decades, Uyghurs have observed that Chinese authorities have gradually removed the Uyghur language from science-related subjects in K-12 schools and universities in Xinjiang.

→ Every scientist needs to study Xi's speeches and thoughts.

Their Western counterparts may not be able to empathise with this but imagine a group of physicists or astronomy professors sitting in a conference room at MIT or Harvard, studying Donald Trump's or Joe Biden's speeches, and then considering how much it would help in their research.

Some 11 years after Xi's rise to power, Xi Jinping Thought Institutes/

LEFT: Dr Gao Yaojie arriving in New York in 2007. She finally settled in the USA in 2009 after being constantly harassed in China for her research into blood contamination

Ayup also compared Nurmamat's case to that of Tashpolat Tiyip, a prominent Uyghur geographer and former president of Xinjiang University, where Nurmamat completed his bachelor's and master's degrees.

Tiyip disappeared in 2017, four years before Nurmamat's arrest, while travelling from Beijing to Berlin for a scientific conference. Since then, there has been no information on his whereabouts or the charges against him.

"Even the Xinjiang University website has removed his record from its list of historic presidents, though it still lists a former president who fled to Taiwan in 1949," Ayup noted.

Dangers of US education

Nurmamat began his doctoral studies in molecular biology at the University of Wyoming in autumn 2009, then moved to the University of California for a fellowship, which he completed in 2018.

During the fellowship, Nurmamat travelled to Xinjiang in summer 2017 for a job interview at Shihezi University. He took his wife, Nurimangul, and their US-born five-year-old daughter, Tumaris, with him to China, in hopes of landing a job back in China after his fellowship.

"At the airport, he was interrogated by Chinese officials, and the Chinese passports belonging to him and his wife were confiscated. Their daughter, who held a US passport, was the only one spared from the interrogation," a friend said.

After weeks of questioning, Chinese authorities allowed Nurmamat to return to the USA to finish his fellowship but imposed strict conditions: His wife and daughter, an American citizen, had to stay in China.

"He was also required to promise that he would return to China once his fellowship concluded," the friend added.

Dangerous return

Following the completion of his fellowship in 2018, Nurmamat voiced significant apprehensions about returning to China.

"I'm still really worried. Shihezi University keep asking me to return; but I'm scared to return after my experience in the last summer," he confided to his friend in the USA via a messaging app on 11 April 2018, a screenshot of which was shared with us. "My family wasn't able to join me. I'm hoping they will be able to get their passport back and join me in the USA."

Despite these fears, Nurmamat returned to China in summer 2018, aiming to secure the release of his wife, a Xinjiang University graduate. She had been under house arrest since 2017 and was later detained in an internment facility, known as a "vocational training centre," which holds over a million Uyghurs, according to his friend.

> No one outside the Chinese government knows his location or the length of his sentence, similar to other cases involving Uyghur intellectuals

"Nurmamat thought that keeping his promise to the Chinese authorities would help free his wife and their US-born daughter," the friend said.

But instead of returning directly to Xinjiang, where his wife was detained, Nurmamat took a research position at Tongji University in Shanghai. He believed Shanghai would be safer and hoped to eventually reunite with his family. But his efforts proved futile, as he eventually followed the path of other Uyghur intellectuals before him, with arrest and detention.

Kasim Abdurehim Kashgar is a Uyghur journalist covering China. This is an edited version of an article that was originally published by Voice of America (VOA)

Centres have been set up in every province and in every prestigious university. The number of such institutions may now exceed 1,000. They employ battalions of scholars, spend buckets of money and publish a vast number of papers every year.

On the website of Tsinghua University, under the label "scientific research", we can find what kind of research some so-called scientists are doing: "Research on the Historical, Theoretical, and Practical Logic of the Communist Party of China's Advancement of Theoretical Innovation in the New Era"; and "Research on the Theoretical Construction and Empirical Evidence of the Party's Self-Revolution to Lead the Social Revolution".

It's not a surprise to learn that these projects are all fully funded by the government. Equally unsurprising is that there are many, many worse papers produced at less prestigious universities.

These papers are also widely cited, but it is clear that the number of citations is not enough to prove their quality. Even truly scientific papers may need to be scrutinised more closely in terms of what they are about, where they are published, whether they have been carefully read, and by whom have they been cited. According to 2023 research from the Institute of Japan's Ministry of Education, Culture, Sports, Science and Technology, 61% of citations to Chinese scientific papers come from within China.

As for China's science and technology patents, according to a 2014 report, former Chongqing police chief Wang Lijun held an astounding 254 of them, including for a shirt, a hot pot and some odd-looking tables and chairs. At the height of his power, he averaged a new invention every 1.7 days, and even China's official media later admitted that his inventions were "nothing to be praised" and neither was he much of a scientist or inventor. His achievements were related to only one thing – his →

ABOVE: A student at Tsinghua University, Beijing, China

→ power. Not everyone has such power, therefore they can't hope to achieve the scientific success that Wang Lijun has.

Most scientists are living on the edge of their seats. A university physics teacher told me that his life is like "a mouse caught by Schrödinger's cat" – he doesn't know if he's going to die, or how and when he's going to die. It is getting more difficult for scientists to access foreign academic websites, and sometimes they cannot even use Google because other Chinese scientists have helped the government build the Great Firewall, which blocks many media and academic websites as well as personal websites and blogs. In recent years, scientists have been forced to reduce their communication with their foreign peers and refrain from commenting on public affairs, including in private gatherings. Even in

their own classrooms they adhere to the commandment that "silence is golden" because, as is commonly said: "everyone knows, some students are not coming here to learn, they are looking for opportunities to turn you in".

What happens if a person does not remain silent?

Teachers are driven out of their classrooms, doctors lose access to their patients, researchers are no longer able to do their research.

If they speak up a little louder, they end up like Gao Yaojie, one of China's most famous doctors. She was expelled from her hospital, placed under house arrest, saw her family implicated, and finally had to flee China.

She died alone in a New York City apartment because of her exposé of the Aids scandal in China caused by commercial blood transfusions.

If anyone has the audacity to publicly criticise the Communist Party or Xi, they will suffer this same fate – such as that of physics professor Ye Qisun or his student Xiong Dazhen, who were arrested, abused and executed half a century ago.

Such a country is not a paradise for scientists and is likely to become their torture chamber – or, at least, force them to become Schrödinger's mice.

Such a country is destined not to contribute much to science, which requires questioning, not unconditional obedience, and open minds, not imprisoned brains. Professor Stephen Sass, who taught in China, argued before his death that if it did not change its policy of suppressing dissent and censoring speech, it would be unlikely to lead in innovation anytime soon.

My perspective is even more pessimistic. If Xi continues to rule in this way, it won't be long before

China becomes a poor and backward country again.

Whereas 50 years ago every Chinese person needed to learn Mao Zedong Thought, which guided everything from the raising and killing of pigs to the treatment of mental illnesses, now everyone needs to learn Xi Jinping Thought. I shudder to think where it will lead.

Another friend of mine who is a university physics teacher in China is also thinking about emigrating because of an incident during a public lecture a few months ago.

When talking about the black hole theory, he offhandedly brought up the critique of the theory by the Chinese scientific community – in fact, by the government – 50 years ago.

"At that time, the black hole theory was considered idealistic, but it was later proved," he said.

There was a clever kid in the lecture theatre who raised his hand and asked: "Teacher, you're talking about the Cultural Revolution, right? Do you think such a mistake would happen again?"

My friend reacted very quickly: "No, no, no, it wasn't a mistake, it was just a normal scientific argument."

He hurriedly ended his talk, and was in a state of shock afterwards, saying: "Luckily, I was quick, otherwise…"

He was so close to committing a terrible mistake, as Xi's regime had explicitly ordered that no "historical errors of the Party" may be taught in university classrooms. He was also sure that there were some snitches among the students, as well as believers of Western pseudo-history.

"You know, it's a genuine black hole," he said. "It swallows everything. Even light cannot escape." ✖

Murong Xuecun is one of China's most celebrated dissident writers, and author of Deadly Quiet City: Stories From Wuhan, Covid Ground Zero

CREDIT: Lou Linwei/Alamy

The uneducated peasants and the rural cadres all believed that Einstein was a bourgeois lapdog

53(03):46/50|DOI:10.1177/03064220241285701

Scriptures over science

SALIL TRIPATHI looks at how science in India is being distorted to fit the prime minister's populist agenda

ON 5 SEPTEMBER 2014, within months of his election as India's prime minister, Narendra Modi addressed high school students. It was India's annual National Teachers' Day.

When an earnest student asked Modi about the climate crisis, he first made some paternalistic comments about children being so clever these days. Then he added that the climate was not changing, we were changing.

This presumably philosophical or metaphysical response had little to do with science and more with Modi's preference of uttering meaningless bons mots.

India is one of the biggest emitters of carbon and has a huge responsibility to protect the planet, and the girl's question was hardly absurd – but Modi made light of it.

Scientists were aghast, but Modi's base – the Hindu nationalist voters yearning for a clever strongman – lapped it up.

That remark was an early indicator of Modi's perfunctory interest in science. He likes to wave the tricolour when India lands a spacecraft on the moon's south pole, but he gives free rein to his officials, who appoint underqualified religious fundamentalists who make outlandish and outrageous claims at institutes of technology.

For example, first-year engineering students at the Indian Institute of Technology in Mandi will now have to study a required course in topics including reincarnation, near-death and out-of-body experiences, and theories of consciousness.

The rot begins at the top, and Modi is prone to making scientific claims that simply don't stand up.

He has said he used a digicam and email in 1988 – when the first commercially viable digicam wasn't invented till 1990, and the use of email (or data transfers) was highly restricted and certainly not available to the general public until the 1990s.

After he ordered airstrikes in Pakistan in early 2019 to retaliate against an attack in India, Modi claimed he told the air force that rain and cloud cover would help Indian aircraft avoid detection by Pakistani radars. That would be news to air traffic controllers around the world, who seamlessly enable landings and takeoffs during terrible weather.

He has puzzled over the mathematics behind $(a+b)^2$ for more than five years and has even claimed that genetic science began in India – and that plastic surgery existed in prehistoric, mythical times. How else did the elephant-headed God Ganesha have his head transplanted?

Such hilarious assertions are a feature of Modi's Hindu nationalism. Taking a cue from the sustained assault on rationality and science, officials have gone about rewriting educational curriculums with abandon, undermining the future of Indian students.

Last year, the science journal Nature reported that Indian school textbooks for 15 to 16-year-olds were removing lessons on the periodic table and evolution. The textbook authority said the topics were removed because they were covered elsewhere, or because they were "difficult".

Modi's ministers have also frequently criticised the evolution theory, refusing to accept that humanity descended from apes.

One minister falsely cited the late scientist Stephen Hawking, claiming he had called the *vedas* (ancient religious texts) superior to Einstein's $E = mc^2$. Modi's ministers have lavished resources on spurious research – such as the National Institute of Hydrology being asked to investigate whether Mount Kailash, in the Himalayas, is the source of the Ganges, as Hindu mythology claims.

To improve farm yield, farmers are asked to practise "yogic farming", where they meditate so that seeds can feel "positivity".

And Shankar Lal, a leader of the right-wing group Rashtriya Swayamsevak Sangh, praised how the application of cow dung to his mobile phone protected him from harmful radiation. "Cow is our mother," he told The Indian Express. "Its excreta and urine are nectar and have power to save humans from any disease. If cow dung can treat cancer, why can't it save us from a phone's microwaves?" Remind me not to borrow his phone even to make an emergency call.

To be sure, Indians love wallowing in nostalgia and seek solace from ancient achievements, since much of the life →

 Shankar Lal … praised how the application of cow dung to his mobile phone protected him from harmful radiation

ABOVE: A scientist at the Clinigene Medical Research Center Bangalore, India

→ around them shows misery – potholed newly-built roads, new trains being derailed and leaking parliament and airport buildings.

The veneration of ancient wisdom has picked up since the Bharatiya Janata Party came to power, and Vedic Mathematics is another topic Indians have written extensively about. While there is a lot to learn from ancient mathematics, especially in abstract aspects, there is also a lot of noise, including leaps of logic.

Even the prestigious Indian Science Congress is not immune from nonsense, as "chauvinistic claims" are getting made.

In 2019, the vice-chancellor of Andhra University, who is an organic chemist, asserted that Kauravas, the villainous cousins of virtuous Pandavas in the Sanskrit mythological epic Mahabharata, were test-tube babies, and that Ravana, the Lanka king whom Rama defeats in Ramayana, had aircraft.

Another scientist insisted that Sir Isaac Newton and Albert Einstein were misinformed, and that gravitational forces would be renamed "Narendra Modi waves".

Other claims made at such ostensibly scientific gatherings included that Pythagoras' theorem was invented in India, not Greece; that there were interplanetary planes during the Vedas; that cows can turn their food into gold; that a helmet from the time of the Mahabharata was found on Mars; and that autopsies can be conducted by leaving a dead body on water.

There have also been claims that the aeroplane wasn't invented by the Wright brothers but by a homegrown talent, and that an Indian had tested a nuclear device in ancient times, as a minister told a flabbergasted parliament.

Unsurprisingly, the Cambridge-based Nobel laureate Venkatraman Ramakrishnan, who has headed the Royal Society, has called the Indian science congress "a circus", and other Indian scientists are in despair.

There are shrewd business reasons for making the alternative reality respectable. Ramdev, a yoga instructor who fashions himself as a holy man and calls himself Baba Ramdev, owns a large ayurvedic medicine business called Patanjali.

He misses no opportunity in criticising modern medicine and sought an injunction against a critical book about him by journalist Priyanka Pathak-Narain. His multi-billion-dollar business has been frequently challenged for making bizarre claims – the Supreme Court recently pulled him up – but the Modi establishment likes him.

A year after Modi became prime minister, Ramdev was an honoured guest at the Indian Institute of Technology.

These incidents seem as if they are from a Monty Python sketch. It would be funny if it wasn't so serious.

The cynical purpose behind it is to convince a resurgent, assertive India that it had always been a superpower. Its Hindu faith, Vedic knowledge and ancient philosophy gave it unparalleled wisdom.

Things went south when Muslim invaders conquered India and then the British colonised the country and subjugated Indians. In the years after, India dithered and fumbled, achieving little. It was only when Modi came to power that India took its rightful place.

This fanciful narrative is absurd and

Even the prestigious Indian Science Congress is not immune from nonsense

false, but it works for two reasons. One, Indians old enough to remember the independence movement or the prime ministership of Jawaharlal Nehru (1947-64) are dwindling fast. And two, Indians born after 1992, the year the BJP's foot-soldiers destroyed the Babri Masjid in Ayodhya, outnumber those who were born before 1992. That mosque destruction fundamentally changed the ethos of India, as it began to transform – slowly at first, rapidly later – into a Hindu nation.

Attacking Nehru, the real builder of modern India, has been a priority. Not only because of his genuine popularity worldwide, easy familiarity with international norms and his erudition but also because he steadfastly opposed irrationality and obscurantism.

Promoting "scientific temper" was Nehru's priority, and he ensured that one of the articles of the constitution required that the state did just that.

It was in his time, and that of his immediate successors, that India built centres of excellence such as the institutes of technology, space research, atomic energy research, engineering, pure sciences and applied sciences, institutes studying cellular and molecular biology, and laboratories for physical research. It also promoted nuclear science and invested in boosting agricultural production.

Those advances helped India beat droughts, the Green Revolution fed millions, Indian rockets began orbiting the earth, and the country's satellites provided connectivity and improved weather forecasting.

In the 1980s US companies discovered the potential of operating from India while engineers slept in the USA, with Indian programmers working on software code. As the Indians went to sleep, their American counterparts

took over, creating a seamless 24-hour cycle. Little wonder that writers such as Angela Saini rightly extolled the good that the "geek nation" could do.

But these developments came at a cost. India's rigid caste system ensured that access to quality education was for upper castes, and upper castes resented the government's affirmative action quotas extending opportunities to disadvantaged groups.

Nehru's early focus on elite institutions of higher education also meant that basic, primary education did not receive sufficient investment. So India had the dubious honour of having a very large number of skilled scientific personnel and engineering talent as well as an extremely large number of people who were actually, or functionally, illiterate.

Downgrading modern science and cheering hoary traditions is a fine, feelgood activity, but India needs to question if it can afford such a luxury. Decrying proven science and established theories and allowing pseudoscience to prevail would create a generation of zombies who would know how to forward rumours on WhatsApp but lack the intellectual means to understand if those rumours had any truth.

That requires one to know reason and begin to doubt. These are the cornerstones of a scientific mind, and it flourishes in an environment that respects freedom of inquiry and expression.

But these ideas can destabilise an insecure government. And that explains why Modi and his ministers want Indians to follow scriptures and not peer-reviewed papers. ✖

Salil Tripathi is Index's South Asia contributing editor

53(03):51/53|DOI:10.1177/03064220241285702

A catalyst for corruption

POURIA NAZEMI explores why being a scientist in Iran is so dangerous, and what is left behind when advancement is hindered

RAN, A COUNTRY that in its distant past played a significant role in the development of knowledge and laid the foundations upon which modern science now stands, has experienced a tremendous urge for scientific rebirth over the past century.

But Iranian scientists are facing a government that considers itself the manifestation of God's will on Earth, that has no qualms about intimidation and oppression, and whose daily rhetoric revolves around the word "enemy".

It wants its ideological model to be seen as the path to success and is terrified of criticism, quickly making everything from nuclear energy and the space industry to vaccination and public medical services into a security issue.

It may be no surprise that Iran's nuclear programme is now securitised, and that the Supreme National Security Council demands silence or compliance from science and media institutions. The tool of national security has now become a pressure point in Iran for any thought that does not align with the government's ideology.

I have covered science and technology news in Iran for more than 10 years. Although I've dealt with issues that were considered red lines on multiple occasions, the only time my colleagues and I received a death threat was when I published a story about the importance of blood transfusion and rejected the

unscientific and dangerous practice of *hijamat* (cupping therapy – a form of Islamic traditional medicine). But that incident is in no way comparable to the deadly consequences of censorship that occurred during the Covid-19 pandemic.

When the pandemic was claiming lives, the supreme leader of the Islamic Republic, Ali Khamenei, banned the entry of vaccines from the USA and the UK into Iran. This was a decision that cost many lives.

The reaction of domestic media to this decision was silence under censorship, and when foreign media reacted they were accused of being agents of the enemy.

"You won't find even one media outlet asking what the consequences of the leader's decision were in this regard," said one doctor and medical science activist, who asked to remain anonymous.

"Even Dr [Masoud] Pezeshkian, who is himself a physician, at that time – before his presidential election – when asked about the vaccine, said we didn't want to import vaccines from certain countries based on our policy, although he was surely aware of the effects of this decision."

While Iranian-made vaccines had not yet received their controversial approval, and parts of the Food and Drug Agency in the Ministry of Health were trying to enforce minimal oversight, the Ministry of Intelligence accused three scientists

and managers of co-operating with the enemy and obstructing the approval of the vaccine.

It requested that the judiciary prosecute them.

Correspondence showing this was revealed only in a set of documents published by a hacker group called Ali's Justice after it gained access to Iran's judiciary.

In this correspondence, it was mentioned that, due to the matter's sensitivity, the case should be investigated without informing the public or arresting the individuals. A few days later, the Barakat vaccine was approved in Iran.

Pressuring individuals active in scientific fields has a long history in Iran.

After the protests following the 2009 presidential election results, known as the Green Movement, several professors who supported them were expelled from universities. There were similar incidents after the events of the Woman, Life, Freedom movement.

In late January 2018, the intelligence agency of the Islamic Revolutionary Guard Corps arrested several environmental activists involved in a project to save the endangered Asiatic cheetah. The Tehran prosecutor accused them of espionage.

But a panel including ministers of justice and lawyers announced that they had found no evidence of espionage. Even the Ministry of Intelligence stated that it had no evidence to support the charges.

One of those arrested was conservationist Kavous Seyed-Emami, a Canadian citizen. Two weeks after his arrest, prison authorities informed his

> Contrary to popular belief that scientists are always pure and honest people, they, too, are subject to this corruption

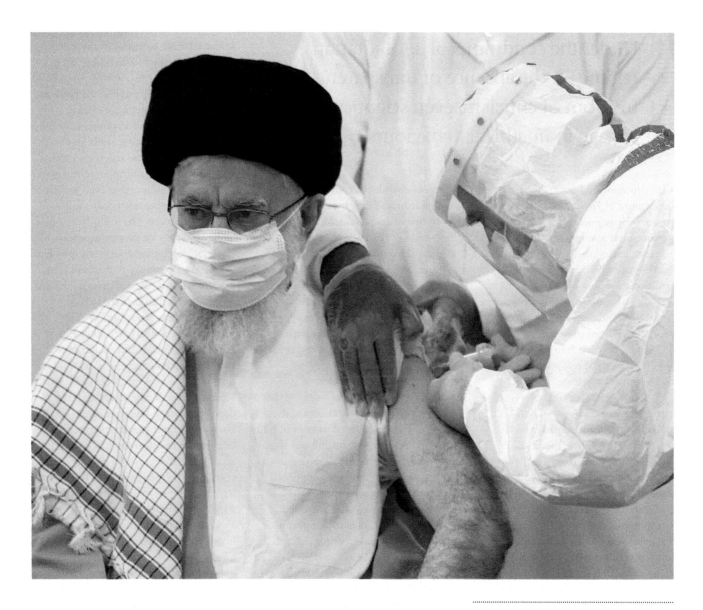

ABOVE: Iranian supreme leader Ayatollah Ali Khamenei receives a locally made Covid-19 vaccine

family that he had killed himself.

However, his family believe that his death was due to physical injuries resulting from torture in prison, and signs of beating were visible on his body.

Another detainee was forced to confess on state television, and others served their sentences in full. Finally, after enduring six years of imprisonment without any evidence of the reasons for their arrest, the remaining detainees were released in April as part of a pardon.

Blocking the flow of information

One of the methods researchers used during the pandemic to estimate the actual mortality rate from Covid-19 and expose the discrepancies in official statistics was to refer to the monthly birth and death statistics published by the National Organisation for Civil Registration.

Mahan Ghafari, a virology specialist at the University of Oxford who followed this issue, told Index how, after the reports were published, the organisation restricted and stopped publishing this data. Eventually, access to the organisation's website was blocked for those outside Iran.

Another part of this pressure involves halting international collaborations. Ghafari recalls how, after a paper was published with an Israeli co-author, the Iranian regime accused all the scientific findings of being a plan against Iran by Israel.

Scientists working on Iran-related issues from outside the country face the risk of harassment. Even their travel to Iran and visiting their families is affected, so many prefer to stay silent.

In the wave of arrests of environmental activists, Kaveh Madani, who at the time was the deputy →

Under the conditions of a totalitarian regime, in the absence of transparency and freedom of criticism, even scientists may engage in unethical behaviours.

→ for education and research at the Department of Environment, was also arrested. He repeatedly spoke about security interrogations and the review of his communications by security agencies.

Although the official reason for his arrest was not announced, his explicit warnings about Iran's water bankruptcy and the impending water crisis were widely considered to be a driving factor.

Madani later left Iran and was appointed as the director of the UN think-tank on water.

The story of Madani's arrest is often cited as a cautionary tale. When globally recognised Iranian experts return to help improve the situation in Iran, they not only have to battle the complex bureaucracy of the political structure but also face unaccountable political entities. They risk interrogation, arrest, imprisonment and even death. This situation only exacerbates the self-censorship among Iranian scientists living abroad.

An Iranian-American researcher currently working in cosmology, who asked not to be named, told Index about another aspect of structural censorship and the pressures it creates.

"I would love to do things alongside my professional work that bring science into people's homes – lectures, talks with the media, sharing my experiences. However, due to the fear of being targeted by political groups inside the country and the limitation on my ability to travel to Iran, I have completely stopped these activities. This fear halted great opportunities that could have been used to promote science and help Iran's scientific development," they said.

They also pointed out how Iranian scientists outside the country faced dual pressures. While the security environment and censorship prevent them from criticising a scientific project in Iran, they are deprived of many research opportunities elsewhere because of their Iranian background.

Their funding is sometimes denied if they have dual nationality, and they face more difficulties in advancing in the scientific community of their host country.

Powerful but chaotic censorship

When protests over the killing of Mahsa (Jina) Amini sparked the flames of the Woman, Life, Freedom movement in Iran, students and academic institutions were not spared from the assault. Not only were students attacked and suppressed, professors who raised their voices in support of them were also repressed.

Encieh Erfani, an assistant professor of physics at the Institute for Advanced Studies in Basic Sciences in Iran, resigned in 2022 in protest against the regime's treatment of students and is now continuing her scientific activities outside the country. She told Index about the wider issues.

"The problem here is that the censorship structure has red lines that you know exist and, from experience, you know you should not even come close to them," she said.

What Erfani points to is one of the most significant reasons for the intensification of self-censorship in Iran. The fear of unknowingly crossing red lines leads to conservatism in the scientific community – a community that can grow only by pushing existing boundaries.

Kiarash Aramesh, director of the Pennsylvania Western University's James F Drane Bioethics Institute, which focuses on biomedical sciences and the humane treatment of patients, agrees. He recently published a book on pseudoscience in medicine in Iran.

"As long as you don't oppose the principles of Islamic traditional medicine, you can publish your articles. But the scientific institution in Iran is so influenced by politics that even within the scientific community there will be opposition to you," he said.

Beyond slowing down the process of scientific development, censorship in Iran is creating a corrupt environment from which anti-scientific and pseudoscientific trends emerge and thrive.

"When there is corruption in society, there is also corruption within the scientific community. Contrary to popular belief that scientists are always pure and honest people, they, too, are subject to this corruption. Under the conditions of a totalitarian regime, in the absence of transparency and freedom of criticism, even scientists may engage in unethical behaviours and participate in corruption for personal gain. Just as we have seen in history, this story repeats itself," Erfani said.

Censorship in science in Iran is a many-faced monster that, on the one hand, forces scientists within the country into conservatism and, on the other hand, tries to ideologise the structure of science through threats and intimidation.

It has discouraged and prevented many Iranian scientists abroad from participating in scientific discourse and contributing to its development in Iran. It restricts international collaboration between Iranian and non-Iranian scientists and it creates a dark space for the growth of corruption – a situation exacerbated by the repression and threats against science media and free scientific journalism. ✖

Pouria Nazemi is a science journalist who was born in Iran and now lives in Canada

53(03):54/56|DOI:10.1177/03064220241285703

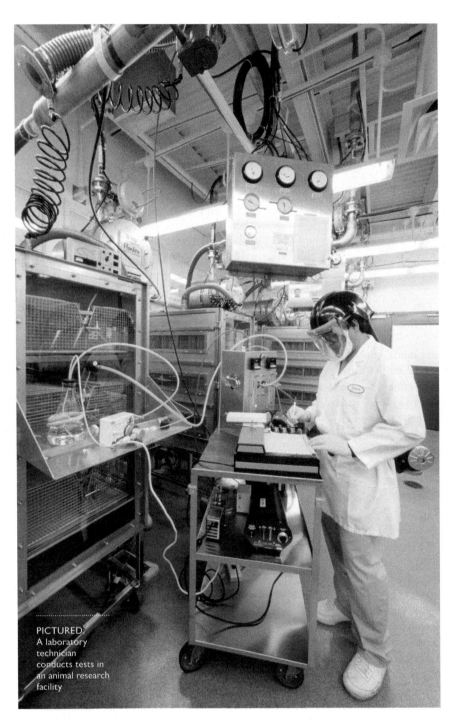

PICTURED:
A laboratory
technician
conducts tests in
an animal research
facility

SPECIAL REPORT ◆ INCONVENIENT TRUTHS

Tainted scientists

KATIE DANCEY-DOWNS talks to the scientists who have been
censored for questioning the effectiveness of animal testing

LISA JONES-ENGEL NEVER envisioned
being thrown out of a conference
hours before she was due to give a
keynote speech. But that's exactly what
happened when she told the organisers
of an event for scientists involved in
animal testing about her new role with
the non-profit People for the Ethical
Treatment of Animals (Peta).

The first reaction to her announcement
had been "Maybe don't come to dinner
with us tonight in case anyone asks what
you're doing," along with an instruction
to remove the Peta reference from the
cover slide of her presentation. All the
other slides were approved.

Jones-Engel is a former primate
scientist who spent years running
tests on monkeys and is now working
to eradicate the use of primates in
biomedical research, but she was not
there to talk about her work with Peta.

With her keynote due at 9am, she got
a text at around 7.15am asking her to
meet the organisers downstairs.

"There's the three of them plus the
chair, and then they said, 'Leadership has
decided that you can't do this,'" she told
Index. They took her security badge.

Jones-Engel thought there had been
a mistake. She was a senior scientist.
She'd given this exact talk before on
international stages. Holding in the
tears, she took the lift back to her room.
Within minutes, there was a knock at
the door.

"They're confused. They're coming
here to say they're sorry," she remembers
thinking. Instead, it was security, there to
escort her out of the hotel.

"I've basically just been cast out as
a scientist, as far as I can tell," she said.
"What the industry did that day was to
guarantee that they had just solidified
who I am and who I was going to be."

Bias in the lab
A number of scientists told Index
that they were being refused funding
or publication if they questioned the
validity of animal-based methods, and
that association with animal advocacy →

LEFT: A long-tailed macaque inside Ubud sacred monkey forest, Bali

→ groups made them toxic in the world of academia. They claim others are afraid to speak up.

Some of these scientists are part of the Coalition to Illuminate and Address Animal Methods Bias (COLAAB), an international coalition of researchers and advocates addressing a crucial issue: that animal methods are still considered a necessity within medical testing, even when better science is available. Emily Trunnell, a USA-based neuroscientist, is part of the coalition and the director of Peta's Science Advancement and Outreach division.

"What we are interested in is when scientists who use only non-animal methods either submit manuscripts or submit grant applications, and are asked by the reviewers to add in an animal test to a study that's otherwise completely non-animal or are rejected because they didn't include an animal test," she explained. "What ends up happening is that the true value of these non-animal methods becomes suppressed."

Until recently, this phenomenon was anecdotal but a survey by scientists including Catharine Krebs, who leads Colaab, now shows the scale of the problem. Out of 90 survey respondents, 31 had been asked by peer reviewers to add animal experiments to their non-animal studies. Survey respondents came from around the world.

"You cannot validate non-animal methods using animals – that's just not scientific," said Frances Cheng, chief scientist in the Laboratory Investigations Department at Peta, explaining that animal data was being valued more than data based on human physiology.

Charu Chandrasekera was an animal researcher until two things drove her to change: the ethical implications, and "realising firsthand the colossal limitations of animal research".

She explained that scientists could reduce animal testing drastically with already available technology, and she demonstrated this by showing Index an organ-on-a-chip, which simulates the responses of a human organ.

Now, she is the executive director of the Canadian Centre for Alternatives to Animal Methods at the University of Windsor, which promotes human biology-based tests. But when she was trying to establish a centre for

alternatives, the response she got from the dean of science at one university was: "You've got to be kidding me. I don't want to offend the animal researchers here."

She told Index there was a culture within the scientific community that disregarded human data as anecdotal, and required that scientists validated human data with animal models.

"The system is set up in a way that you can't really fight it if you want to have a career in academia," she said. "You have to publish or perish. You depend on these funding agencies to give you the money, and they're requesting animal data."

Chandrasekera has experienced this bias herself. When she applied for a grant to develop a 3D bio-printed human lung tissue model, one of the biggest criticisms from the peer review was a lack of animal data.

"And guess what I did? I said, 'Keep your money!'" She went on to secure private funding, but she added: "Not everyone has the means to fight against the system."

She knows scientists who support animal-free methods but stay silent. They are worried about the implications when they sit in front of grant review panels and journal editorial boards.

Dismissing activists
Jones-Engel said there was a group of scientists who functioned as activists and received silencing treatments like she did before her cancelled keynote speech.

"It seems that in other disciplines we accept scientist activists. We accept climate scientists who are activists. We accept physicians who advocate for their patients, who are activists about

 I've basically just been cast out as a scientist, as far as I can tell

maternal rights. But within the animal research community, that is somehow considered anathema," she said.

She has seen colleagues choosing not to speak up about the use of primates in laboratories because they don't want to be seen as activists.

When Cheng questioned the use of animals during her training, she was not trying to highlight animal cruelty but rather that the methods were unscientific, with animal biology not translating to human biology. When she wrote a line in the dedication of her thesis apologising to the animals she'd unnecessarily killed, her supervisor told her to remove it, as it would lower her chance of graduation. She was told her job was to graduate, not to think about animal cruelty and translatability. Now, Cheng keeps a tally of all the animals she's saved compared with the ones she's killed, so that she can see on paper that the results are net positive.

Once she'd graduated, she knew she did not want to work in the animal testing industry, and she volunteered at a hospital doing clinical research. The role of co-ordinator of clinical trials became available, and her supervisor was supportive of her application. She waited for a response, and then she received an email from her supervisor, asking her to join him on a walk in the woods, away from monitored communications.

He'd been told by the second-in-command that they couldn't hire Cheng because she was an animal rights activist.

"At that time, I really wasn't," she said. "I think the only thing that was public was a photo that people took of me at a circus protest, and it was on my Facebook account, and it was set private, so the only way that they would know is if they'd hacked into my account somehow."

The second-in-command went on to tell her supervisor: "You know we do animal research, right?"

More recently, Cheng tried to submit a science-based commentary on issues with using mice and rats for human

Scientists could reduce animal testing drastically with already available technology

nutrition research but was rejected by the reviewers because of her affiliation with Peta.

For Trunnell, when deciding whether to accept the job at Peta, she said: "I felt like the decision I was making was whether or not I was OK with being blacklisted in science in order to pursue this goal." Ultimately, she doesn't feel that has happened, but she remembers the assumption within the animal research community that activists were blacklisted.

The monkey in the room

In 2022, Jones-Engel was part of a group of scientists who did an assessment for the International Union for Conservation of Nature (IUCN) on the long-tailed macaque, the most widely traded species used in laboratories, finding that the species which was once everywhere in Southeast Asia was now facing a dramatic decline.

The IUCN consequently moved the monkeys to "endangered" status. Since then, she said, there had been a move by the industry to dismiss the idea that the macaques were really disappearing.

The National Association for Biomedical Research, a US non-profit which calls itself the "national voice for animal research ", submitted a petition to the IUCN against the listing.

Jones-Engel told Index: "I was personally attacked. A petition was written by the industry targeting me, another scientist and another activist saying that, even though we're scientists, because we are advocating for the listing of those animals to be endangered that must mean this was all being driven by the animal rights community."

The monkeys have remained on the endangered list, and Jones-Engel said that although CITES (the Convention

on International Trade in Endangered Species) could have done more, they had kept the countries supplying macaques on a review list.

There is huge money behind animal research. Cheng explained that animal tests were often used to produce health claims for food and drink, and at the moment those tests were cheaper than clinical tests.

Jones-Engel added that for companies known for using or supplying animals, there was a fine balance if they wanted to move towards non-animal testing.

"How do you not spook your shareholders? How do you not scare your investors?" she said.

Chandrasekera said there was an entire industry which benefitted financially from animal testing, from selling mice to providing specialised instruments. They have an interest in animal tests continuing.

There have been huge developments globally in phasing out chemical testing on animals, and there is a scientific community moving away from using animals in labs. But the larger percentage, Chandrasekera said, did not want to change or were scared to do so.

She makes a stark point. While these scientists are silenced, the advancement of medicine suffers. We do not have effective treatments for a huge number of diseases, and without the acceptance of better models that translate to human biology, that can't change.

"Federal funding agencies and scientific journals of the 21st century must stop acting like the Catholic Church of the 15th century, which silenced and persecuted brilliant minds." ✖

Katie Dancey-Downs is assistant editor at Index

53(03):57/59|DOI:10.1177/03064220241285704

Death and minor details

Pathologists in Uganda are being stopped from uncovering the truth behind mysterious deaths, writes **DANSON KAHYANA**

EATH SHOULD BE a natural occurrence, but there are situations when it happens unnaturally – a car crash or a natural disaster, for example. Those who are bereaved usually understand both scenarios.

What they do not understand is where the death is sudden.

The Ugandan state is known to be heavy-handed in dealing with citizens who belong to opposition political parties, and a "sudden" death is usually considered the "dirty job of the state".

The implication is that the opposition politician (as they often are) has been eliminated through either physical violence or bio-chemical means. And pathologists are not always allowed to investigate properly.

Claims that poison is used as a way of dealing with dissent have become common in Uganda.

When Jacob Oulanyah, speaker of the 11th Parliament, died on 20 March 2022, his father, Nathan Okori, claimed that his son had been poisoned. The official cause of death, according to the Ugandan parliament, was multiple organ failure related to cancer.

Stella Nyanzi, one of president Yoweri Museveni's most articulate critics, published a poetry collection on this subject that she provocatively entitled Eulogies of My Mouth: Poems for a Poisoned Uganda.

When Cerinah Nebanda, the opposition member of parliament representing the women of Butaleja District, died at the tender age of 24 on 14 December 2012, the entire country was astonished by the news since she was so young, and in very good health.

New Vision, a pro-ruling party daily newspaper, reported that a government chemist had found "cocaine, heroin, alcohol and several other chemicals" in her blood, gut and tissue samples.

Nebanda's colleagues did not agree with these findings, so the speaker, Rebecca Alitwala Kadaga, sent the country's most renowned and experienced forensic pathologist, Sylvester Onzivua, to South Africa with the samples to conduct a confirmatory autopsy.

On 18 December 2012, Onzivua was arrested at Entebbe airport and charged with abuse of office on the grounds that he was illegally and unlawfully in possession of the late parliamentarian's body parts.

This disturbed Nebanda's relatives and colleagues, who asked: "If the state had nothing to hide regarding what caused Honourable Nebanda's death, why has it blocked Dr Onzivua from flying to Pretoria?"

Nebanda's mother was unequivocal in her castigation of the state.

She told mourners: "The state knows who or what killed my daughter. This is why they arrested the pathologist that my daughter's colleagues at the parliament had hired to seek a second opinion in South Africa."

The country's first lady, Janet Kataaha Museveni, responded by telling

ABOVE: Dr Sylvester Onzivua was arrested before trying to perform an autopsy

the mourners that Nebanda was not the regime's biggest critic, so the state could not have done what it had been accused of.

Onzivua remained in police custody for two days, after which he was released on police bond (where an arrested person is released until the police complete their findings). After nine months, the courts threw the case out as the police did not have evidence that he had stolen the sample he was taking to South Africa. To allay fears that the state had a role in the death of Nebanda, the Ministry of Health claimed that it had done a confirmatory autopsy outside the country, in Israel, but people remained sceptical as there were questions the state could not convincingly answer.

First, why had it chosen to take the sample to Israel and not South Africa,

The state knows who or what killed my daughter. This is why they arrested the pathologist

the country where parliament had sent Onzivua? Second, why was the state now doing the confirmatory autopsy, yet it had hounded Onzivua for trying to do the same thing?

Finally, why was Onzivua not involved in carrying out the confirmatory test in Israel, since he was the one parliament had tasked to do the work?

The entire saga affected Onzivua's work with his employer, the Ministry of Health, and Mulago National Referral Hospital, his workplace. Although he was the most senior, experienced and renowned pathologist in the country, his services were more or less dispensed with since he was not given new assignments.

"I was put on what Ugandans call *kateebe*," he told Index, using the Luganda word for "little seat", a phrase used in Uganda's military to refer to officers who have not been given assignments.

"I continued receiving my salary, but I was not scheduled to carry out autopsies. You could say that my superiors at the Ministry of Health and at Mulago Hospital ostracised me because I was seen as serving interests antithetical to the ruling party."

He added that his arrest had tainted his reputation, and said: "I was framed as an unethical and criminal person who had stolen the body parts belonging to a dead woman."

The state had communicated a powerful message. If it could beat the best trained, most experienced and most renowned forensic pathologist in the country into a tight corner, what chance did the lesser-trained, lesser-experienced and lesser-known pathologists have?

When Onzivua turned 60, the mandatory retirement age in Uganda, in December 2023, he hung up his forensic tools. Although he was one of a very small team of pathologists in the country, he knew that he did not have

a chance of getting a post-retirement contract since he was a marked man. The state had practically shut down his forensic laboratory.

Poison continues to be mentioned in several deaths in Uganda, but it is a subject that the state does not entertain. Onzivua knows why.

"All over the world, death is sensitive – especially if there are criminal or political overtones at stake. For this reason, the state does everything within its power to manage the narrative of the cause of death," he said.

Several other high-profile people are rumoured to have died of poison, including Brigadier Noble Mayombo, who died in May 2007 while serving as permanent secretary of the Ministry of Defence and Veteran Affairs; the popular Muslim cleric Sheikh Nuhu Muzaata Batte, who died in December 2020; and Hussein Kyanjo, former member of parliament for Makindye West, who died in July 2023.

In 2015, David Sejusa, a general in the Uganda People's Defence Forces, informed the nation that there was deep mistrust among members of the cabinet to the extent that people carried their own food and drink to meetings and state functions to avoid being poisoned. Media outlets including the Daily Monitor and the Observer quoted the general as saying: "We who are inside the

army, inside cabinet, inside parliament – you cannot serve me tea and I take it."

The state has learnt to manage the rumours better, even threatening to arrest those who utter the word "poison".

But some dissidents manage to communicate the fear that they could be poisoned or murdered. One of these, Herbert Anderson Burora, former resident city commissioner for Rubaga Division in Kampala City, took to X in April after he was fired for condemning corruption in the ruling party that he served.

He wrote that if he were to die, people should "never believe that I died of a heart attack or multiple organ failure", and that any accidents must be properly investigated.

"Heart attack or multiple organ failure" is how pathologists' reports from government hospitals read. "A car or motor accident" is how police reports usually read when a dissident dies. Burora's post critiques the falsification of both pathologists' and police reports that is censorship as practised in Museveni's government. ✖

Danson Kahyana is a poet, author and scholar at Harvard Kennedy School, Stellenbosch University and Boston College. He is Index's contributing editor for East Africa

53(03):60/61|DOI:10.1177/03064220241285705

RIGHT: People set to work making coffins in Kampala, Uganda

The dangers of boycotting Russian science

JP O'MALLEY talks to exiled scientists about the difficulties of continuing their work

MIKHAIL VIKTOROVICH FEIGELMAN started working at the Landau Institute for Theoretical Physics in Moscow in 1980. Eleven years later, when the Soviet Union collapsed, funding and decent modern equipment were rare for Russian scientists but there was suddenly intellectual freedom.

"This is why I stayed in Russia at this time, despite the hardships," the 70-year-old physicist told Index. "This freedom during the 1990s was very important, but it didn't last long."

In May 2022, just months after Russian President Vladimir Putin launched a full-scale invasion of Ukraine, Feigelman fled to western Europe.

"I left exclusively because of the war," he said. "I could no longer live in Russia anymore, where I see many parallels with Nazi Germany. I will not return home until the death of Putin."

Initially, Feigelman took up a position at a research laboratory in Grenoble, France, where he stayed for a year and a half. Today, he is employed as a researcher at Nanocenter in Ljubljana, Slovenia.

"I have not experienced any prejudice or discrimination in either France or Slovenia," he said.

"But in Germany – at least in some institutions – there is a [ban] on Russian scientists, and it is forbidden to invite them for official scientific visits."

These measures stem from a decision taken by the European Commission in April 2022 to suspend all co-operation with Russian entities in research, science and innovation.

That included the cutting of all funding that was previously supplied to Russian science organisations under the EU's €95.5 billon research and innovation funding programme, Horizon Europe.

The boycotting had already begun elsewhere. In late February 2022, the Journal of Molecular Structure, a Netherlands-based peer-reviewed journal that specialises in chemistry, decided not to consider any manuscripts authored by scientists working at Russian Federation institutions.

One former employee at the journal, who wished to remain anonymous, said Russian scientists were always welcomed to publish in the journal. "A decision had been taken, for humanitarian reasons, after Russia's invasion of Ukraine, not to accept any submission authored by scientists (whatever their nationality) working for Russian institutions," they said.

Last January, Christian Jelsch became the journal's editor. "This policy to ban Russian manuscripts was implemented by the previous editor," he said. "But it was terminated when I started as editor."

Feigelman believes all steps taken "to prevent institutional co-operation between Europe and Russia are completely correct and necessary."

But he added: "Contact from European scientists with individual scientists must be continued, as long as those scientists in question are not supporters of Putin."

Alexandra Borissova Saleh does not share that view.

"Boycotts in science don't work," she said. "There is a vast literature out there on this topic."

She was previously head of communication at the Moscow Institute of Physics and Technology and head of the science desk at Tass News Agency in Moscow.

Today, Borissova Saleh lives in Italy, where she works as a freelance science journalist and media marketing consultant. She has not returned to Russia since 2019, mainly because of how scientists are now treated there.

"If you are a top researcher in Russia who has presented your work abroad, you could likely face a long-term prison sentence, which ultimately could cost you your life," she said.

"But the main reason I have not returned to Russia in five years is because of the country's 'undesirable organisations' law."

First passed in 2015 – and recently updated with even harsher measures – the law states that any organisations in Russia whose activities "pose a threat to the foundations of the constitutional order, defence or security of the state" are liable to be fined or their members can face up to six years in prison. This past July, The Moscow Times, an independent English-language and Russian-language online newspaper, was declared undesirable by the authorities in Moscow.

"I'm now classed as a criminal because of science articles I published in Russia and in other media outlets," Borissova Saleh explained.

Shortly after Putin invaded Ukraine,

I hope Cern will continue to keep these channels open to reduce the risk for nuclear war happening

an estimated 7,000 Russian scientists, mathematicians and academics signed an open letter to the Russian president, voicing their public opposition to the war.

According to analysis carried out by the Russian newspaper Novaya Gazeta, since February 2022 at least 2,500 Russian scientists have left and severed ties with Russia.

Lyubov Borusyak, a professor and leading researcher of the Laboratory of Socio-Cultural Educational Practices at Moscow City University, carried out a detailed study of Russian academics included in that mass exodus.

Most people she interviewed worked in liberal arts, humanities and mathematics. A large bulk of them fled to the USA and others took up academic positions in countries including Germany, France, Israel, the Netherlands and Lithuania. A common obstacle many faced was their Russian passport.

It's a bureaucratic nightmare for receiving a working and living visa, Borusyak explained.

"Most of these Russian exiles

abroad have taken up positions in universities that are at a lower level than they would have had in Russia, and quite a few of them have been denied the right to participate in scientific conferences and publish in international scientific journals."

She said personal safety for academics, especially those with liberal views, is a definite concern in Russia today, where even moderate, reasonable behaviour can be deemed as extremist and a threat to national security.

"I feel anxious," she said. "There are risks and I'm afraid they are serious."

Hannes Jung, a retired German physicist believes it's imperative scientists do not detach themselves from matters of politics, but that scientists should stay neutral when they are doing science.

Jung is a prominent activist and co-ordinator for Science4Peace – a cohort of scientists working in particle physics at institutions across Europe. He said their aim was "to create a forum that promotes scientific collaboration across the world as a driver for peace".

ABOVE: Former Russian Prime Minister Dmitry Medvedev (centre) meets with Russian scientists in 2019 at the European Organization for Nuclear Research (Cern). Four years later, Cern officially announced it was ending co-operation with Russia and Belarus as a response to the "continuing illegal military invasion of Ukraine"

He helped form Science4Peace shortly after Russia invaded Ukraine in 2022, as he felt the West's decision to completely sever ties with Russian scientists was counterproductive and unnecessary.

"At [German science research centre] Desy, where I previously worked, all communication channels were cut, and we were not allowed to send emails from Desy accounts to Russian colleagues," said Jung. "Common publications and common conferences with Russian scientists were strictly forbidden, too."

He cited various examples of scientists working together, even when their respective governments had ongoing political tensions, and, in some instances, military conflicts. Among them is the Synchrotron-light for Experimental Science and Applications →

LEFT: Current Russian Prime Minister Mikhail Mishustin (right) visits the Institute of Electric Propulsion of the Moscow Institute of Physics and Technology (MIPT) in the Moscow region.

→ in the Middle East (Sesame) in Jordan: an inter-governmental research centre that brings together many countries in the Middle East.

"The Sesame project gets people from Palestine, Israel and Iran working together," Jung said.

The German physicist learned about the benefits of international co-operation among scientists during the hot years of the Cold War.

In 1983, when still a West German citizen, he started working for Cern, the European Organization for Nuclear Research. Based on the Franco-Swiss border near Geneva, the inter-governmental organisation, which was founded in 1954, operates the largest particle physics laboratory in the world. At Cern, Jung was introduced to scientists from the German Democratic Republic, Poland and the Soviet Union. "[In] the Soviet Union the method for studying and researching physics was done in a very different way from in the West, so there was much you could learn about by interacting with Soviet scientists," he said.

In December 2023, the council of

Cern, which currently has 22 member states, officially announced that it was ending co-operation with Russia and Belarus as a response to the "continuing illegal military invasion of Ukraine".

Jung believes Cern's co-operation with Russian and Belarussian scientists should have continued, saying there was no security risk for Cern members working with scientists from Belarus and Russia.

"There is a very clear statement in Cern's constitution, explaining how every piece of scientific research carried out at the organisation has no connection for science that can be used for military [purposes]," he said.

In June, the Cern council announced it would, however, keep its ongoing co-operation with the Joint Institute for Nuclear Research (JINR), located in Dubna, near Moscow.

"I hope Cern will continue to keep these channels open to reduce the risk for nuclear war happening," said Jung.

Can cultural and academic boycotts work to influence social and political change? Sometimes.

They seemed to play a role, for

example, in the breakup of apartheid South Africa (1948 to 1994). This topic was addressed in a paper published in science journal Nature in June 2022, by Michael D Gordin.

The American historian of science argued that for science sanctions to work – or to help produce a change of mindset in the regime – the political leadership of the country being sanctioned has to care about scientists and science. "And Russia does not seem to care," Gordin wrote.

His article pointed to the limited investments in scientific research in Russia over the past decade; the chasing after status and rankings rather than improving fundamentals; the lacklustre response to Covid-19; and the designation of various scientific collaborations and NGOs as "foreign agents", which have almost all been kicked off Russian soil.

Indeed, Putin's contempt and suspicion of international scientific standards fits with his strongman theory of politics. But such nationalist propaganda will ultimately weaken Russia's position in the ranking of world science.

Borissova Saleh said trying to create science in isolation was next to impossible.

"Science that is not international cannot and will not work. Soviet science was international and Soviet scientists were going to international scientific conferences, even if they were accompanied by the KGB," she said.

Sanctioning Russian scientists will undoubtedly damage Russian science in the long term, but it's unlikely to alter Russia's present political reality.

Authoritarian regimes, after all, care about only their own personal survival. ✖

Science that is not international cannot and will not work

JP O'Malley is a freelance journalist

53(03):62/64|DOI:10.1177/03064220241285706

CREDIT: Sipa US/Alamy

Putting politics above scientific truth

DANA WILLBANKS, of the Climate Science Legal Defence Fund, explains why the Silencing Science Tracker they set up at Columbia University is so necessary in the USA today

SINCE THE 2016 presidential election, the USA has seen a rise in the number and severity of attacks on scientists, particularly from within the government.

This anti-science movement has had the effect of silencing critical voices from the scientific community as its members face harassment, abuse and personal and professional threats from those hoping to slow or prevent scientific progress. Funding cuts, political interference, censoring or altering research findings and other tactics have all been used to sow distrust in – and ultimately suppress – science.

In turn, this has reduced public trust in science and has had a profoundly chilling effect on scientists' ability to conduct their vital research and exercise their right to free speech.

In early 2018, the Sabin Centre for Climate Change Law at Columbia University and the Climate Science Legal Defence Fund created the Silencing Science Tracker. This database built on the organisations' existing partnership and overlapping missions of addressing climate change through advocacy and education.

The Sabin Centre also launched a similar database in response to then US President Donald Trump's administration's efforts to diminish the federal government's climate mitigation efforts, and the tracker was specifically designed to document the administration's staggering number of widespread attacks on science.

Following the 2020 election, president Joe Biden promised to keep science at the forefront of his administration. Data from the tracker, however, shows the disheartening reality.

While the Biden administration has undertaken markedly fewer anti-science actions, it has been slow to undo earlier damage – damage that, in some cases, it continues to perpetuate. Moreover, anti-science efforts continue at state and local levels.

As of July 2024, the tracker has documented 531 cases of censorship, information suppression, misrepresentation of scientific facts and other policy or administrative anti-science actions in the USA.

The tracker includes any action by a government entity that restricts scientific research, education, discussion or the publication or use of scientific findings.

Government censorship, the category with the most violations – 167 and counting – includes subverting scientific information by making it difficult or impossible to find, often by changing official websites or publications.

Under the Trump administration, for example, the Department of Agriculture (USDA) was ordered to remove references to "climate change" from official documents, webpages and the agency's Climate Hubs website.

Sometimes, government censorship goes beyond modifying public materials to suppress scientists' free speech, preventing them from speaking about matters integral to public health and safety.

In 2017, staff in the Natural Resources Conservation Service unit of the USDA – whose mission is to support agricultural producers' conservation efforts – were told to use other terms in place of "climate change". That same year, Environmental Protection Agency (EPA) staff were warned that speaking publicly about their work without undergoing multiple levels of review could result in disciplinary action.

And in September 2020, the Trump administration pressured the Centres for Disease Control and Prevention to edit or delay the release of the weekly Covid-19 Morbidity and Mortality Weekly Reports to align with the administration's messaging concerning the pandemic and its use of unverified and dangerous "cures" such as hydroxychloroquine to treat it.

Instances of government censorship have also been documented at state level. In January 2021, New York governor Andrew Cuomo told reporters at one of his daily Covid-19 briefings that he did not "really trust the experts".

Soon after, it was reported that his administration excluded public health experts from pandemic response planning and vaccine rollout efforts and that many state health officials found out about major pandemic policy changes during news conferences.

The second most populated category on the tracker concerns the bias and misrepresentation of scientific findings, such as cherry-picking data to support a political purpose, disregarding findings when crafting public policy, or disclosing only those findings that support a certain conclusion. ➜

 This disregard for science has real and devastating consequences

PICTURED: Young people march in Michigan, USA as part of the Global Climate Strike in 2019 while Donald Trump was president

→ Despite overwhelming scientific evidence and consensus to the contrary, Trump's secretary of energy and Trump himself questioned the human causes of climate change, stating that "scientists say a lot of things" and "I don't think science knows, actually".

This disregard for scientific reality is evident through the tracker. For example, in January 2020, Trump and his top advisers dismissed scientists' and biodefence experts' warnings about the risks of Covid-19. Trump told his secretary of health and human services to "stop panicking" before downplaying the situation to reporters by asserting that it was "going to be just fine".

As more than one million

When the government ignores science, it's like a truck driver who wears a blindfold and drives based on what is whispered into his ear

American families know firsthand, this disregard for science had real and devastating consequences.

These are just a few of the many egregious examples of attacks on science that have been documented.

Other examples include the misrepresentation of medical science as it relates to abortion, such as the Texas Department of State Health Services suggesting that abortion causes breast cancer; several state legislatures passing laws that force doctors to tell their patients that medication abortions can be reversed; funding cuts at federal agencies to research studies and to programmes such as the EPA's Children's Health Research Programme; and the termination of advisory committees and the disbanding of scientific panels.

The sustained attack on scientists and the chipping away of public trust in science have had serious impacts on public health, environmental protection and climate change mitigation efforts, both at home and abroad.

While the USA was once considered a world leader in science and innovation, the continued prioritisation of politics over truth has damaged that standing – perhaps irreparably so.

Heartbreaking firsthand accounts reveal the deep personal harm caused by the anti-science movement. People whose homes have been destroyed by extreme weather events, those who have experienced medical emergencies that leave lasting damage, and those who have lost loved ones to Covid-19 have suffered the consequences of a government prioritising political gain over the wellbeing of its people.

When sitting members of Congress publicly declare that masks and vaccines do not slow the spread of Covid-19, people listen – with devastating results.

While these shorter-term impacts on scientific research and public policy are well documented, the long-term impacts will reverberate for years to come.

With the prospect of the return of another anti-science administration, we are once again highlighting this tool to remind us all of the ongoing fight against misinformation.

We know that it has an impact. The Silencing Science Tracker has been referenced in congressional hearings and reports and in letters by members of the Senate and the House of Representatives.

Along with other work we do in support of stronger federal scientific integrity policies, the tracker helps bring attention and, therefore, positive changes to anti-science measures that might otherwise go unnoticed.

Scientists and others who have witnessed or experienced these attacks have bravely come forward to share their stories. These accounts bring home the personal and professional repercussions that too many in the scientific community face when simply trying to perform and publish their research.

As Michael Gerrard, founder and faculty director of the Sabin Centre, said at the launch of the tracker: "When the government ignores science, it's like a truck driver who wears a blindfold and drives based on what is whispered into his ear – dangerous and intolerable."

It is critical that we all call out efforts to silence science, do our part to protect scientific freedom and integrity, and remove the blindfold of ignorance and apathy. ✖

Dana Willbanks is the communications co-ordinator for the Climate Science Legal Defence Fund.

53(03):65/67|DOI:10.1177/03064220241285707

The science of purges

KAYA GENÇ speaks to two Turkish academics and finds that persecuting scientists is by no means a new phenomenon

ON 20 JULY 2016, five days after a failed coup attempt in Turkey, the country's president, Recep Tayyip Erdoğan, declared a state of emergency and began issuing a set of emergency decrees known as KHKs. On 7 February 2017, he issued a KHK to "cleanse" Turkish academia of scientists that Erdoğan claimed were "linked to terror", purging 330 scholars.

Since then, "KHK" has become a scary term among intellectuals and scholars. In newspaper articles and official correspondence, a terrifying suffix ("has KHK") was added to the names of the unlucky ones prosecuted under Erdoğan's decrees.

"They should be treated as suffering civil death," one pro-government columnist argued: a loss of all civil rights and the inability to obtain any employment in the future.

Over the next eight years, about 1,000 scientists would suffer this fate. Many had their passports confiscated and, in some cases, were imprisoned simply because Erdoğan linked their names, without evidence, to terrorism.

But after opposition parties began to triumph in local elections, first in 2019 and then in 2024, the courts started to find the courage to resist Erdoğan's ruthless purges. By 2021, numerous courts ordered Turkey's most respected scientists to return to their jobs.

But the public universities, run by Erdoğan's cronies who are afraid of the strongman's fury, refused to renew the contracts of leading scientists. Instead, administrators ordered further investigations to be conducted against them. In a ceaseless struggle to show their fealty to Turkey's hegemon, university rectors appointed by Erdoğan even asked scientists to pay back the salaries they had received since returning to their jobs.

The violent purging of Turkey's scientists by Erdoğan has created an academic diaspora in Europe and the USA.

Yet this kind of treatment of scientists is by no means a novelty in Turkey.

Professor Öget Öktem Tanör, 89, was Turkey's first neuropsychologist. She told Index how the state had continually persecuted her and her husband, Professor Bülent Tanör, who died in 2002.

Her struggles began half a century ago when the Tanörs had to flee to Switzerland in the wake of a failed coup, a counter-coup and a military memorandum issued on 12 March 1971.

"My husband and I encountered all these pressures repeatedly," Tanör said. They were purged in 1983 during another period of repression, and in 2001 after a professor who was involved in a coup in Azerbaijan was appointed rector of Istanbul University. Both were punished for representing academics unhappy about the rector's appointment, but as the case was going through the courts, Bülent Tanör died.

In 2017, 15 years after losing her husband and after becoming a professor, Tanör was again in trouble, this time charged with "terrorism propaganda". In January 2016, she signed a petition calling on the government to halt its military operations in eastern Turkey.

The number of signatories snowballed from 1128 to 2212 in a week, and the government quickly opened court cases against signatories. Three signatories were sent to jail. Numerous others lost their jobs and suffered "civilian deaths" during the 2017 KHK purges.

Aged 82, Tanör was threatened with the prospect of losing her civil service pension rights and her Green Passport (issued to civil servants and giving them rights to travel visa-free round Europe). She had already retired and worked for the private Science University (Bilim Üniversitesi).

"After I became a professor, I never encountered pressure from the university until I signed this petition for peace," Tanör said. "Because the government [hasn't cancelled] my KHK, I'm no longer considered a public servant and can't get a Green Passport. My father was the education minister; even that doesn't make me eligible. When they look at my name, they see this note: "She has KHK, so she can't get a Green Passport."

Tanör believes the problem has become systematic in Turkey, but if the political regime were to change tomorrow things would be fixed rapidly. "The justice system would return to normal, and the separation of powers would be restored. At the moment, the executive wields all the power. Just one person decides everything. When things change, independence will come to the judiciary, and science and universities will benefit from independent-minded authorities."

 The violent purging of Turkey's scientists by Erdoğan has created an academic diaspora in Europe and the USA

Numerous things have changed beyond repair under Erdoğan's two-decades-long reign, she said, ("like agriculture and farming because of all the damage inflicted on these") but justice and universities can "can much more easily return to good health".

Bülent Şık, a food engineer who once worked at Akdeniz University as the deputy director of the Food Safety and Agricultural Research Centre, is another scientist victimised by Erdoğan's purges.

In the 2010s, Şık worked on a five-year research project commissioned by the Health Ministry to investigate possible relations between high cancer rates in western Turkey and soil, water and food toxicity. He reported his findings to the government but heard nothing back.

In 2016, Şık signed a petition that called for peace between Turkish forces and Kurdish militants. He was one of those scientists branded "has KHK" the following year. He lost his university position as an assistant professor.

"Even before the KHK, universities were in bad shape in conducting scientific studies and notifying the public through scientific articles or statements," Şık told Index.

"In 2012, while working at Akdeniz University, I conducted a study on toxic chemicals in food. We found alarming results about their effects on children's hormonal and neurological development. I summarised the report and shared it as a press statement, highlighting the problem and pointing to precautions that needed to be taken."

Şık was unnerved to receive a call from a high-level bureaucrat at the Ministry of Agriculture. "He called me on my phone, asking me to withdraw my comments. He said my comments left the ministry in a challenging position."

The bureaucrat threatened to go to the press and tell them that Şık had confessed to making false statements to the media. But Şık wouldn't budge.

When he was purged in 2017, Şık learned that university administrators

had received calls from the Health Ministry. "They told me: 'You had already caused so much trouble with the Health Ministry and put the university administration in a tight spot.'"

While there is a list of all the purged scientists, we don't know about those who have been bullied, Şık warns. "Because of bullying, so many scientists feel forced to retire or don't get their contracts renewed."

The void left behind by purged scientists is easy to observe. In the past three years, Turkey has experienced one of the most severe food and nutrition crises in its history, with food prices rocketing. Yet little scientific inquiry is made about this.

"The abnormality resembles the World War II era," said Şık. "The

skyrocketing food prices resulted in great food insecurity. Around 100 departments in Turkish universities study food as an academic subject. No report or study has been published about how the children have been affected by this crisis. This tells us something."

It's not only active censorship that leads to this deafening silence. "The more important factor is self-censorship among scientists. They mostly think something could happen to them due to their reports or that the pressures can interfere with their academic promotions," Şık said.

Worse, scientists who live under autocratic regimes such as Turkey's can, in time, "lose their ability to see what is important to study for the public good". Şık likened the current state of Turkish →

→ university administrations to ones he observed at military garrisons. "Higher-ups stop scholars below them, trying to plan their future studies so they won't harm the university administration's good relations with the government."

Eight scientists were purged from Akdeniz University with Erdoğan's KHKs. Two couldn't return to their posts (they're now appealing to a higher court), but six were eventually reinstated. Şık returned in February 2024. He hadn't severed ties with his department staff and said his former students, who were now working on their PhDs, "celebrated my return like a festival".

Yet soon afterwards, Şık learned that university administrators had appealed to a court to get him fired again.

What Şık felt during the second

BELOW: Istanbul University is among the institutions that have purged academics

Higher-ups stop scholars below them, trying to plan their future studies so they won't harm the university administration's good relations with the government

attempt to purge him from academia was different. "We had struggled for many months to stand tall and return to our posts. We were reinstated and then, in just three months, the university wanted us gone again," he said.

And he expects to be expelled again.

"Honestly, I can see no future for me in the university," he said. He has now applied for retirement.

Şık said scientists should always ask themselves why they are doing science even, or perhaps especially, when facing pressures from strongmen such as Erdoğan. "It doesn't matter if you're

a young scientist or someone devoted decades to the field. You can do science to improve the world or just for career reasons. Sadly, the science world in Turkey is increasingly choosing the latter."

Şık believes Turkey's public universities are beyond repair. "You can work at the lab and design projects only if the system allows you. If they keep on sabotaging your projects, what's the point?" ✖

Kaya Genç is Index's contributing editor for Turkey

53(03):68/70|DOI:10.1177/03064220241285708

SPECIAL REPORT ◆ INCONVENIENT TRUTHS

The fight for science

UK Journalist **SIMON SINGH** won a landmark legal battle calling out "bogus treatments", but as Index's **MARK STIMPSON** discovered scientific truths are still being contested

FIFTEEN YEARS HAVE now passed since the publication in the UK of an article about science, or rather pseudo-science, which kicked off an expensive legal battle and ended, five years later with the reform of Britain's libel laws.

An article in the Guardian, Beware the Spinal Trap, written by scientist and author Dr Simon Singh, took aim at

chiropractors, particularly those who promoted the therapy as a way of treating virtually any ailment or illness, not just the back problems. Singh had explored the claims of chiropractors in his book Trick or Treatment, co-authored with Edzard Ernst, an expert in the study of complementary and alternative medicine.

In the article, Singh wrote: "The British Chiropractic Association [BCA]

ABOVE: Simon Singh at the Royal Courts of Justice after winning his appeal against the British Chiropractic Association

claims that their members can help treat children with colic, sleeping and feeding problems, frequent ear infections, asthma and prolonged crying, even though there is not a jot of evidence. This organisation is the respectable face of the chiropractic profession and yet it happily promotes bogus treatments."

The BCA strongly objected to the article and sued the author.

Speaking to Index, Singh said: "The article was written by me, read and checked by a medical expert, and checked again by the Guardian comment editor and the Guardian legal desk … and we all thought it was a fair and reasonable article." ➔

→   Unfortunately for Singh, the court case came at a time when scientists and journalists who write about science were coming under attack from organisations eager to polish their reputations, and companies wanting to protect their investments, particularly when it came to drug research.

Tracey Brown, director of campaigning organisation Sense about Science, said that in the 1990s and early noughties there was a growing feeling of openness and transparency among scientists globally. "Access to evidence was open and you had initiatives, for example, to make the body of scientific literature available to people in countries where libraries didn't have the money for subscriptions."

But as the new millennium progressed that optimism died and companies and organisations started to use the UK's libel laws to silence critics.

As Brown explained: "People were being dragged to the London courts or threatened with being dragged to the London courts and silenced that way. To the shock of many in the human rights movement, it was affecting scientists and groups of patients who wanted to debate which treatment worked. It was affecting medical whistleblowers. It wasn't just the oligarchs and their big businesses that were using that technique. The law was being used to effectively to silence scientific discussion.

"Journals were so fearful that it began to affect things like their decision to retract papers and their decision to publish responses to papers. Things were being pulled for no good scientific reason."

It was into this world that Singh's article appeared. In a preliminary hearing in 2009, Justice Eady ruled that the use

of the phrase "bogus treatments" was a statement of fact rather than an opinion, which Singh denied. As a result, he faced ruin. Costs in the case amounted to more than £200,000 and he had been unable to work while defending the case, resulting in two years of lost earnings.

Despite this, Singh took the expensive decision to take the decision to the Court of Appeal. A year later, it ruled that Singh's remarks were fair comment. After Singh's successful appeal, the BCA withdrew its action.

Singh's case and the libel laws

Following the ruling, Index along with Science about Science and English PEN joined forces to launch the Libel Reform Campaign. It attracted tens of thousands of supporters, including Stephen Fry and David King, former chief scientific adviser to the UK government.

This resulted in the 2013 Defamation Act which made sweeping changes to the law including the granting of privilege to scientific journals for articles and statements which had been peer-reviewed; a requirement that plaintiffs must demonstrate they had suffered serious harm following publication; and a stronger defence of fair comment.

Singh would have been extremely unlikely to have been taken to court for his article under such a law.

Singh told Index: "I am quite happy with how events unfolded, from the failure of the British Chiropractic Association's case against me to the reform of the libel laws, so I would certainly write the same article again, assuming it would lead to the same sequence of events."

But while Singh was ultimately successful he still rues the "chilling effect of libel".

ABOVE: Dr Simon Singh lost two years of earnings and faced costs of more than £200,000.

"For every article that provoked a libel action, there were hundreds of others that were written in an overly cautious manner, skirting around the real issues, just in case a single contentious word could lead to a multi-million pound libel bill," he said.

Overall, Sense about Science's Tracey Brown believes the success of the Libel Reform Campaign was positive too and says there were other spin-offs from the campaign.

People were being dragged to the London courts or threatened with being dragged to the London courts and silenced that way

CREDIT: Robert Sharp / English PEN surname#

"What we learned from the Libel Reform Campaign, we put to direct use in the huge international campaign for Alltrials [the initiative to ensure all clinical trials are reported], which was very successful in highlighting the fact that fewer than half of the trials on the drugs people use were ever published. And guess what? Generally speaking, it was the half that companies didn't want you to know about that were not."

She highlights the case of a drug whose efficacy has been effectively enhanced because trials where the drug failed to perform are hushed up. "The integrity of the research base and the basis for deciding what works in future medicines was really questionable," she said.

"If you have a drug to tackle stroke risk and someone comes along with a compound that is better, you don't see it's better because you're comparing it with something that's too optimistic in the first place. There may well have been things that haven't been developed and haven't been brought to market because they're being compared to over-optimistic interpretations of the drugs we've already got."

Science being silenced

While the reform of the libel laws helped science get a fair hearing, it has still not ended the attempts to silence science in the UK.

A study by the University and College Union in 2017 found that more than 35% of academics have undertaken self-censorship (refrained from publishing, teaching or doing research on a particular topic), for fear of negative repercussions; the figure was 19% in the EU.

Covid, with its waves of scientific claims and counter-claims, was a particular low point argued Brown. →

ABOVE: Scientists Chelsea Polis (left) and Nancy Olivieri (right) pick up the 2023 Maddox Prizes from Sense about Science director Tracey Brown (centre).

→ "During the pandemic, we saw cases where companies were threatening researchers and the universities lawyers were encouraging those researchers to simply withdraw their comments and promise never to repeat them," she said.

The annual Maddox prize, run by Sense about Science in conjunction the scientific journal Nature exists because of attempts to silence scientists round the world. The prize recognises courageous individuals who stand up and speak out for science and evidence-based policy, advancing public discussion about difficult topics despite challenge or hostility. Prize-winners have often called out the intimidation of researchers and the organisations which have failed to protect them.

"It's really important for society that researchers can be confident to talk about their findings, especially when they are not what we expect or raise difficult questions. When decisions are made without all the evidence, we all lose out," says Dr David Schley, Sense about Science's deputy director.

In 2023 the prize went to Nancy

Olivieri, now a senior scientist at Toronto General Hospital in Canada. In 1998, Olivieri blew the whistle over the drug deferiprone, used to remove excess iron from the body in patients with thalassaemia major, which was being trialled at the hospital in where she was then working. Olivieri suspected the drug was causing serious adverse events, which the drug manufacturer and trial funder Apotex denied. When Olivieri said she intended to inform participants of her concerns, Apotex terminated the trials and invoked a confidentiality agreement in the research contract and threatened legal action if she made the findings public. Undeterred, Olivieri shared her results at a scientific meeting and submitted them for publication. She was sacked.

In 2009 the FDA declined Apotex's request for approval of deferiprone as first-line therapy. In 2011, the FDA issued approval for deferiprone as "last resort" therapy, to be prescribed only after first-line therapies had failed, cautioning that no controlled trials of deferiprone had demonstrated direct treatment benefit.

"Hostility was certainly a feature of my story: the harassment, the bullying, the multiple firings by academic institutions enabled by a pharmaceutical company over two decades," said Olivieri when she picked up the award.

The role of social media

Social media has also placed scientists in the firing line.

"What worries me enormously is the idea that we can write an algorithm for science," Brown told Index. "What 20

years in this interface between science and society has taught me is that there are no shortcuts. During the pandemic, you had the British Medical Journal and the Cochrane collaboration being unable to publish because the algorithm had been determined that the title of papers fell foul of what was considered good science.

"It misunderstands science; science is about the new; algorithms are based on the past. So inevitably any algorithm will not account for new discoveries."

Academic institutions have also become really dependent on their social media profiles as they try to attract high-fee-paying students from around the world.

"They are really touchy about any kind of bad online publicity," said Brown. What that means is that they really don't have the backs of people who work for them and they often overreact."

Singh argues that social media isn't the only culprit.

"There is a ton of scientific misinformation on social networks, but there is also far too much dodgy material in the mainstream media," he said.

"A sensationalist scaremongering article will always appeal to readers, and a phone-in based on pseudoscience will too often find a home on local radio."

A decade and a half on from the BCA case, Singh has moved on. Since the libel case, he has not written any new books, a shame given his titles on Fermat's Last Theorem and the Big Bang were hugely successful popular science titles.

His focus is now on a charity called Good Thinking, set up to "encourage curiosity and promote rational thinking".

Singh says, "We are pro-science and pro-evidence, which means we are anti-woo and anti-quack. In short, we like scepticism, but not cynicism. We like nerds and geeks, but we hate bogus things without a jot of evidence." ✖

Mark Stimpson is associate editor of Index on Censorship

53(03):71/74|DOI:10.1177/03064220241285709

A study by the University and College Union in 2017 found that more than 35% of academics have undertaken self-censorship

GRANICA PAŃSTWA
PRZEKRACZANIE ZABRONIONE

COMMENT

"This unruly band of comrades has been brought together by the bitter and often lonely struggle against Stalinism, their friendship formed in an underground network of Polish-Czech solidarity."

ANYTHING IS POSSIBLE | MARTIN BRIGHT | P80

On the brink

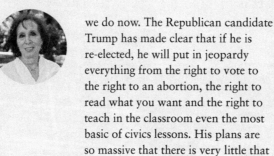

Freedom and democracy are on the ballot in the US presidential election, writes **JO-ANN MORT**

PATRIOTISM HASN'T BEEN a standard stance of the Democrats, and especially not of their left flank. But front and centre issues in this election – freedom and democracy – are two words that have become the mantra of the Democratic standard bearer, Vice President Kamala Harris. There may be many reasons for this transformation, or this embrace, but I would venture that the main reason is that a second Trump presidency is so profoundly dangerous to the notions of democracy and freedom that make the United States the nation that we are. These two notions are intertwined – the American experiment is one that put the citizen at the core of our national experience. Our very citizenry is at risk.

The battle lines are drawn. This will be a close election, way closer than it should be, considering the credentials of the two candidates - Vice-President Kamala Harris and former president and convicted criminal Donald Trump. But America is a divided nation, with a profoundly dangerous fissure among a disenfranchised white working class conjoined with a cynical white business class, versus, well, the rest of us.

It's perhaps extraordinary that we have never since our founding seen our freedom and democracy at risk as we do now. The Republican candidate Trump has made clear that if he is re-elected, he will put in jeopardy everything from the right to vote to the right to an abortion, the right to read what you want and the right to teach in the classroom even the most basic of civics lessons. His plans are so massive that there is very little that will be left off his agenda.

It's important to understand that the Trump candidacy is the tip of a movement in America that seeks to take us backwards. With a Republican party totally in his grip, and a determined activist base, this is an anti-freedom movement that must be squashed so that the United States can fulfill its most basic self-professed promise of democracy.

The blueprint for a second Trump term is found in a massive document called Project 2025 prepared by the right wing Heritage Foundation. Among the policy plans are defunding of the Corporation for Public Broadcasting, shuttering of the Department of Education, so that "education decisions are made by families," along with the gutting of the national public education system.

Abortion of course is at even more risk than it is already, since we are living with the legacy of the first Trump campaign and his packing of the US Supreme Court with anti-choice justices. There is a proposal by the Trump campaign to create a National Anti-Abortion Coordinator while also forcing states to report on women's miscarriages and abortions. (In some states, doctors are already at legal risk for providing health care to pregnant women). He has endorsed using the Comstock Act, a 19th century relic that censors free speech, to enforce abortion by making it a crime to promote or receive abortion pills across state lines.

The freedom to learn is already at risk, also a legacy of the first Trump term. Imagine things to get so much worse if there is a second term. According to PEN, the writer advocacy group, "Since the fall of 2021, PEN America has counted over 10,000 book bans in schools across the country. The full impact of the book ban movement is greater than can be counted, as 'wholesale bans' in which entire classrooms and school libraries have been suspended, closed, or emptied of books, either permanently or temporarily, restricted access to untold numbers of books in classrooms and school libraries. Overwhelmingly, book banners target stories by and about people of color and LGBTQ+ individuals."

This has trickled down into communities all across America. Teachers are afraid to teach in classrooms across the country (see p102). Public school and small town libraries are being stripped of books deemed inappropriate by those who want to limit knowledge. School boards are among the fiercest election platforms, often with groups that appear to be grassroots but are otherwise funded by those allied with the Trumpist movement.

And finally, at risk is that most basic of rights, the right to vote. The USA is already the most repressive democracy in the world regarding access to voting. Under a Trump regime, it will become even more so.

Trump, as we know so well, tried to steal the last election. Now, under plain sight, he and his allies are plotting to do the same - packing electoral panels and trying to manipulate state election laws. There

And finally, at risk is that most basic of rights - the right to vote

will be key challenges in states known as battleground states that could go either Democratic or Republican, like Georgia and Arizona. The arcane system of the electoral college is vulnerable to this manipulation in ways we never have seen before Trump's emergence on the world stage. To challenge this, the Harris campaign has added an army of lawyers. Their immediate focus is to challenge the right to vote in key states where the Trump campaign is litigating against it. The second focus will be on the myriad of challenges that Trump plans to throw up regarding the actual vote count and legitimacy of the vote itself. As the New York Times recently reported: "The battle over whose votes count – not just how many votes are counted – has become central to modern presidential campaigns," as a legacy to the Trump phenomenon.

When the election results are challenged, the deciding bench will be the US Supreme Court, the most conservative and anti-democratic court in our nation's history. Were he to win a second term, his legacy would impact generations far into the future.

Jo-Ann Mort is a writer and democracy activist based in New York, USA

53(03):76/77|DOI:10.1177/03064220241285712

Bad sport

DAISY RUDDOCK speaks to a documentary-maker at the heart of exposing a state-sponsored doping scandal

"IF YOU KNOW you're cheating, you're not really winning."

These were the words of British swimmer Adam Peaty, who was speaking after his relay team finished fourth in the 4x100m medley at the Paris Olympics this summer. His cutting remark was undoubtedly aimed at the two members of the gold medal-winning Chinese team who had previously tested positive for performance-enhancing drugs.

Peaty wasn't alone in his anger. US swimmer Nic Fink called for "more clarity and transparency" from the World Anti-Doping Agency (WADA), while nine-time gold medallist Katie Ledecky also called for change after the New York Times reported in April that 23 Chinese swimmers had tested positive for a banned substance but were allowed to compete in the 2021 Tokyo Olympics just seven months later due to the intervention of top Chinese officials.

One man who understands better than most the lengths states will go to cover up doping in sports is award-winning director Bryan Fogel.

"Victory on a global stage – be it at the Olympic games or an international sporting competition or otherwise – shows strength and power," he told Index. "But it goes way beyond sport or Olympics. It's the nature of governments, of society."

Fogel's 2017 Academy Award-winning documentary Icarus was originally intended as a test of anti-doping policies and procedures in sport, to be conducted with the help of Russian scientist Grigory Rodchenkov in an attempt to expose their inadequacies. Instead, Fogel's

cameras ended up capturing the unravelling of the most sophisticated state-sponsored doping campaign in sports history, culminating with Rodchenkov – fearing for his life and on the run from the Kremlin – testifying that Russia had been conducting doping on a mass scale for years, swapping out athletes' positive drug samples for clean ones.

"Although it's the story of this Russian doping scandal, as we're now learning and as Grigory Rodchenkov already knows, the same thing is and was going on in China. You could probably argue the same thing was going on in multiple countries," said Fogel.

However, for the director, the story of Icarus isn't really about doping in sport but about cheating on a country-wide level and the conspiracy to cover it up.

In the documentary, we witness first-hand how Rodchenkov is targeted by the Russian authorities after admitting to helping dozens of athletes circumvent anti-doping procedures in the years prior to the 2014 Winter Olympics in Sochi during his time as the director of the Moscow Anti-Doping Laboratory. He is forced to seek asylum in the USA and go into hiding, where he remains to this day.

Rodchenkov's predicament throws into sharp focus the sacrifices that whistleblowers make to expose corruption; often, the consequences of such bravery never go away.

"I don't think there is any easy path to being a whistleblower especially when you're taking on governments and massive industries or businesses," said Fogel. "I think the plight of Rodchenkov, who has lived in hiding, under protection, under a new identity for the last seven years now, clearly shows that."

In 2022, Fogel released Icarus: The Aftermath, a follow up to the original which tracks the aftermath of the first, shadowing Rodchenkov for five years as he remains in hiding. The film lays bare the bleak future that awaits many whistleblowers. Although he managed to escape Russia, he can never completely shake his constant paranoia after exposing the state's secrets.

In the documentary, we see the impact this has on Rodchenkov's life and health. He is isolated, separated from his family and friends and spends his days looking over his shoulder, expecting the worst.

His fears are not unfounded: Russia embarked on a smear campaign against the former anti-doping lab head in an attempt to discredit him, sending fabricated messages to WADA implicating him as the ringleader in a scheme to extort athletes and coaches. Investigators soon discovered that the messages had actually been inserted into Rodchenkov's electronic records two years after he had fled the country.

Victory on a global stage – be it at the Olympic Games or an international sporting competition or otherwise – shows strength and power

CREDIT: Lifestyle pictures / Alamy

Although he managed to escape Russia, he can never completely shake his constant paranoia after exposing the state's secrets

ABOVE: Bryan Fogel (right) and Grigory Rodchenkov (left) helped to uncover Russia's major state-sponsored doping scandal in the 2017 documentary Icarus

By risking his life to expose the extent of his home nation's state-sponsored doping campaign, Rodchenkov has also involuntarily provided a case study of just how far authoritarian states will go to conceal the truth.

"The issue is that any time someone comes forward in a capacity like this they're putting their lives in danger, end of story. That's the nature of being a whistleblower," Fogel said.

These issues present a very real obstacle to future whistleblowers

– with such a hostile environment to contend with, they are much less likely to step forward. This is particularly worrying when you consider that the very corruption Rodchenkov and Fogel exposed is still going on.

Fogel's Icarus both serves as motivation to investigate such corrupt practices and a warning of the dangers that may face those who do so. If whistleblowers are targeted, intimidated or inadequately protected from hostile states or organisations, fewer people will be

willing to step forward and speak out about illegal or immoral behaviours. In a world where doping in sport is increasingly common, this is an extremely precarious environment to be cultivating.

Too often, those fighting against corruption are being failed. Fogel understands this as well as anyone: "I think what we've seen over and over and over again, even in this current Olympic Games, is the bad guys win." ✖

Daisy Ruddock is editorial assistant at Index

53(03):78/79|DOI:10.1177/03064220241285713

INDEXONCENSORSHIP.ORG **79**

Anything is possible

As the 35th anniversary of the fall of the Iron Curtain approaches we should remember that democratic change can come very quickly writes **MARTIN BRIGHT**

THERE IS A grainy photograph on the first page of the January 1990 edition of Index on Censorship magazine showing a group of twenty or so smiling friends of various ages. They are dressed in the non-descript shabby style favoured by most European intellectuals of the period. They could easily be mistaken for a group of academics on a field trip if it weren't for the sign in Polish behind them which reads: State Border: Crossing Forbidden.

The picture was taken on 9 July 1988 at a secret location on the Polish-Czech border. This unruly band of comrades has been brought together by the bitter and often lonely struggle against Stalinism, their friendship formed in an underground network of Polish-Czech solidarity. The cause often seemed hopeless and at the time the picture was taken this obscure group of writers and activists could never have imagined that the whole edifice they had spent their lives opposing was about to collapse.

As it turned out, this photograph represented one of the most extraordinary gatherings of dissidents in the whole of the Cold War. Look closely and you can see Václav Havel, the Czech dissident playwright, who would become

ABOVE: The secret 1988 meeting of dissidents included: back row, Mirosław Jasiński (first left), Petr Uhl (second left), Adam Michnik (fourth left), Jan Ruml (first right); middle row, Václav Havel (second left), Anna Šabatová (third right), and: front row, Petr Pospíchal (second left), Jan Urban (third left), Jacek Kuroń (third right) and Ján Čarnogurský (first right)

President of Czechoslovakia just 20 months after the photo was taken. Ján Čarnogurský, a Catholic anti-communist activist, who became the Prime Minister of Slovakia in 1991 is also there as is Jan Ruml, who went on to become the Czech interior minister from 1992 to 1997. Jan Urban led the Civic Forum campaign in the elections of 1990, but decided not to become Prime Minister in the new government. A year on, Jacek Kuroń, known as the godfather of the Polish opposition, would be the minister for employment in the first Solidarity government.

Mirosław Jasiński, a leading member of Polish-Czechoslovak Solidarity became a prominent Polish diplomat. Among them also are opposition journalists Petr Pospíchal and Petr Uhl, who founded the East European Information Agency and Adam Michnik, perhaps Poland's most celebrated journalist, who became the first editor of the independent newspaper Gazeta Wyborcza in May 1989 and later an MP before returning to journalism.

The only woman in the photo is Anna Šabatová who went on to become the ombudsman of the Czech parliament and was the first East European woman to receive the United Nations Human Rights Prize.

No one predicted the events of 1989, the 35th anniversary of which, will be celebrated this year. The first signs came in the spring of that year, when the Polish government and Solidarity reached an agreement to legalise the free trade union and hold elections. In June, the Communists were humiliated at the polls and in August Solidarity's Tadeusz Mazowiecki became Prime Minister. A parallel process in Hungary saw the creation of independent parties in February 1989. By the beginning of May, the authorities had dismantled the barbed wire on the frontier with Austria. The borders of the old Communist bloc started to fray and then come apart at the seams. In September, Budapest announced that East Germans would be given passage through Hungary into Western Europe. Young people across Eastern Europe began to make their way in numbers to Vienna to get their first taste of western

consumer goods and freedom. Then, in November, the movement became irresistible as the Berlin Wall itself crumbled and fell under the weight of sledgehammers. In Czechoslovakia, the Velvet Revolution ushered in the peaceful transition to democracy and by Christmas, the Romanian dictator Nicolae Ceaușescu was gone. Crucially, unlike in 1956 and 1968, the Soviet army did not intervene.

For young people across Europe, these were life-changing events. As a wide-eyed 23-year-old journalist, I travelled across Eastern Europe in December 1989. In East Berlin, I spoke to students loyal to the regime whose world had been turned upside down, who asked me to reassure them about the key role played by the Communist Party of Great Britain in the fight against racism and the National Front. In Leipzig I saw the thousands of people taking part in candlelit demonstrations around the city. In Prague I grumbled to two journalists who worked for the trade union newspaper that there would soon be a McDonald's on Wenceslas Square and witnessed their pure delight as they looked me in the eye and said "Yes!" I remember a mixture of emotions among the people I met: hope and optimism about the future of an undivided Europe, certainly, but also a degree of fear and uncertainty about whether the transition would remain peaceful. Common to everyone though was the feeling of pure surprise. Absolutely no one had expected this, even a year earlier.

Index's founder, the poet Stephen

Spender, captured this feeling well in his speech to English PEN at a party for his 80th birthday on 6 December 1989, published in the February 1990 edition of Index magazine. He suggested that a motto for his kind of writer, opposed both to Stalinism and McCarthyism, should be "the politics of the unpolitical", but asked what the role of such writers should be after the end of the Cold War.

"It is essential to ask this question because we are now entering what less than even a year ago was an almost unthinkable period," he said. "How unthinkable is to me made vivid by recalling that at the beginning of 1989 I remarked to Isaiah Berlin, who, like me, has in 1989 reached his 80th year - he and I each other's oldest living friend - that the one thing I wished to see was the collapse of the dictatorships in the Soviet Union and Eastern Europe. He agreed but said that this would not happen in our lifetimes. Well, now it has happened, and the results are completely bewildering."

How bewildered might Stephen Spender be 35 years later. No one talks about "the politics of the unpolitical" anymore. But those of us who were there in 1989 still remember the sense of surprise that everyone who thought they could predict the future was wrong and that feeling, for a short while, that everything was possible. ✖

Martin Bright is editor-at-large at Index

53(03):80/81|DOI:10.1177/03064220241285714

> The one thing I wished to see was the collapse of the dictatorships in the Soviet Union and Eastern Europe. He agreed but said that this would not happen in our lifetimes.

ABOVE: Hong Kong judges bring in the new legal year in January 2024

Judging judges

A British judge sits on a heavily compromised Hong Kong court because he thinks he can "do good". **JEMIMAH STEINFELD** asks whether this sentiment is laudable – or laughable

IT WAS A statement that was meant to subdue criticism. This June, British KC David Neuberger addressed a panel at the Bar Council's conference in London saying he was going to remain on the Hong Kong Court of Final Appeal (CFA) because his "feeling is that so long as I can do good by being there and so long as I think that I might cause harm by leaving, I want to stay and support my judicial colleagues in Hong Kong and support the rule of law as long as I can".

In early August, his words came back to haunt him.

The CFA unanimously agreed to uphold the convictions of seven human rights defenders who participated in an unauthorised, peaceful 2019 protest in Hong Kong – one of them the media mogul and British citizen Jimmy Lai.

Lord Patten, the last British governor of Hong Kong, was quick to respond, saying: "This unjust verdict is made worse by the fact that Lord Neuberger, a former head of Britain's supreme court, was a party to this decision.

"This is particularly surprising since, when he was a member of the judiciary in Britain, Lord Neuberger was keen to establish that the English common law could accommodate fundamental aspects of human rights protection.

"He was also always keen that judges should be keen to explain their reasoning. In this case, perhaps some of his views on the law changed between the first-class waiting room at Heathrow and the arrival terminal of Hong Kong international airport."

The Independent ran the headline "British judge upholds conviction against Hong Kong activist Jimmy Lai despite link to prisoner rights charity", pointing to the fact that Neuberger is a trustee of Prisoners Abroad, a charity that advocates for British prisoners overseas. Other papers highlighted his role as chair of a legal advisory panel to the Media Freedom Coalition.

The CFA, established in 1997 at the time of the handover, is the highest appellate court in Hong Kong. It was meant to maintain judicial independence, but it had qualifications – the most significant being that Beijing could operate ultimate control over court decisions through a right to "interpret" laws.

In 2020, Beijing imposed a harsh national security law upon the territory which essentially criminalised any form of dissent. In March 2022, the UK government and judiciary jointly announced that active UK judges would withdraw from the CFA.

At the time, justice secretary

CREDIT: Lam Yik, Reuters

Dominic Raab said that "it is no longer appropriate for serving UK judges to continue sitting in Hong Kong's courts".

The decision did not, however, affect retired British judges still sitting.

Two resigned nonetheless, leaving five who said at the time that their continued participation was in the interests of the people of Hong Kong. Two more stepped down this June, a few months after Hong Kong passed another draconian national security law.

"I remained on the court in the hope that the presence of overseas judges would help sustain the rule of law. I fear that this is no longer realistic," said one of them, Lord Sumption.

So three remain: Lord Neuberger; Lord Hoffmann, a former law lord; and Lord Phillips of Worth Matravers, the first president of the UK Supreme Court.

Are they misguided in their approach to justice and the role they can play, assuming they really do mean what they say?

I've grappled with this question myself, having briefly worked in Chinese state media at the start of my career (which at the time was staffed by many who thought they'd hold the mantle for media freedom). I concluded that I was unable to effect change and made a swift exit.

But this idea – that an insider can change the system (an argument trotted out in the business world, too) – is clearly compelling.

"When it comes to toppling tyrants, power and proximity matter," said Marcel Dirsus, author of How Tyrants Fall.

He was writing in The Guardian a year after (private military company) Wagner chief Yevgeny Prigozhin's failed military coup in Russia. One wouldn't want to be on the same side as Prigozhin. He was a ruthless man, motivated by the belief that Russian president Vladimir Putin was making

 # Are they misguided in their approach to justice and the role they can play?

a mess militarily, not by any sense of morality.

For Dirsus, there is an alternative path which doesn't involve supporting people such as Prigozhin or being part of an authoritarian regime's infrastructure.

He says "all tyrants blunder" and when they do, well-executed foreign pressure and support – through helping dissidents and defectors for example – can make the difference, which is exactly what we do at Index.

Intrigued by the idea of how to topple a tyrant, I read "How many people does it take to oust a political leader?" by philosopher David Edmonds, which was written following the stolen election in Belarus in August 2020.

In it he interviews Harvard political scientist Erica Chenoweth, who looks at protest in the context of dictatorships (and curiously calculates that a demonstration has to be a precise 3.5% of the population or more to be successful).

Setting aside grandiose plans to overthrow the Chinese Communist Party and just considering if the British judges can make a positive difference on their own patch, I asked Edmonds about a philosophical framing.

He said we could approach their choice in two ways.

The first is through the prism of consequentialism. Can their actions produce positive outcomes? This can often be hard to judge, Edmonds said. Still, given the recent Lai-and-co trial result, it's reasonable to argue "no" here.

The second is a deontological approach, which suggests that there is more to morality than just the outcome or consequences of an action.

"Where you're dealing with an

obnoxious regime, personal integrity comes into play," he said. "Some animal rights campaigners, for example, object to the philosopher Peter Singer's pragmatic approach to improving animal welfare [which doesn't rule out engaging with factory farms] – they say it's like negotiating with a slave owner to improve the conditions of the slave. 'You should have nothing to do with the slave owner,' they say."

Could similar arguments apply to the British judges? It's clear their reputations have taken a big blow. More than this, many say their very presence on the CFA is a win for Beijing, that they're a fig leaf for an undemocratic state.

"These judges purport to be committed to constitutionalism and human rights, but as Hong Kong's authoritarian regime and court system have systematically infringed on the rights of Hongkongers in recent years, they are now merely lending their, and their nations', reputations to legitimise the crackdown," wrote Alyssa Fong and Samuel Bickett from the Committee for Freedom in Hong Kong in their report Lending Prestige to Persecution: How Foreign Judges are Undermining Hong Kong's Freedoms and Why They Should Quit.

Like Patten's remarks, Fong and Bickett's are damning. And yet they feel justified. Let's consider the case: Lord Neuberger is 76. So, too, is Jimmy Lai.

One sits in jail for his role in peaceful protests, the other in a court that is keeping him there. ✖

Index contacted Neuberger for comment.

Jemimah Steinfeld is CEO of Index

53(03):82/83|DOI:10.1177/03064220241285715

Hay Festival
Hay-on-Wye
Winter Weekend

28 November — 1 December 2024

Book now
hayfestival.org/winter-weekend

Talks

Books

Ideas

Debates

Music

Workshops

Discover a world of different...

CULTURE

"These are things that make you think of
consequences and how that can affect your
whole career, just by reading a book that is
good in one setting but not in another."

PUT DOWN THAT BOOK! | KATIE DANCEY-DOWNS | P102

The good, the bad and the beautiful

Russia's most popular writer **BORIS AKUNIN** (aka Grigory Chkhartishvili) tells **SALLY GIMSON** about his writing, being branded a terrorist and the future for Russia

GRIGORY CHKHARTISHVILI, OTHERWISE known as Boris Akunin, is one Russia's most widely read contemporary writers. His books have sold 35 million copies (by his own estimate) and his historical crime novels featuring the detective Erast Fandorin have been made into TV series and films.

Yet now he is on Russia's register of "terrorists and extremists" and a warrant was issued for his arrest by a Moscow court earlier this year for "discrediting the army", "justifying terrorism" and spreading "fake news" about the Russian military.

His books have been banned, his plays cannot be performed and his website is blocked. How did it feel, I wondered, for a writer to be labelled in this way?

"It feels interesting. It feels as if I haven't lived and written in vain. There is a saying by Confucius: one should live in such a manner that good people would love you and bad people hate you. There are people who love me, people who hate me, the latter ones as we all know are quite bad. Confucius would be satisfied," Chkhartishvili told Index.

He fell out with President Vladimir Putin first over Crimea and left Russia in 2014 after criticising the annexation. He went back once, and it was made clear to him that he was not welcome.

Although he has always been supportive of Ukrainians, helping them when they came as refugees to London, the "terrorist" label and arrest warrant came after a bizarre incident at the end of last year where he was scammed by two Russian "pranksters" Vovon and Lexus who have a history of embarrassing celebrities from Prince Harry to Elton John.

They used deep fake technology to persuade him he was talking over video to the Ukrainian president. He told Cathrin Kahlweit, Süddeutsche Zeitung's correspondent for Central and Eastern Europe at an event in Vienna, that he was convinced it was Volodymyr Zelensky.

"Because it was not a public talk, I told him everything that the Ukrainian government was doing wrong... 'you're doing this and that', like an idiot."

The tape was then edited to make it as incriminating as possible.

Chkhartishvili was born in Georgia, but until his exile had spent most of his life in Moscow. He started his career as a literary editor before moving on to writing in 1998. He's a specialist in Japanese literature and enjoys experimenting with many different forms of writing from populist and literary fiction to non-fiction and drama.

One of his biggest recent projects is his History of the Russian State, consisting of 20 books. "There are 10 volumes of historical facts and analysis in parallel with 10 volumes of historical fiction: novels, novellas, theatre plays," he told Index. "My intention was to explain what really happened and then to make history alive with storytelling. It's 10 volumes which are a 1,000 year history of Russia and 10 volumes of one family's history, generation after generation."

Writing this history has made him understand Russia much better and become more realistic about what might be possible post-Putin.

"Russia must cease being an empire. It is such a huge and diverse country that it can be managed only in two fashions: either by dictatoring [sic] or in a confederalist mode – like Switzerland. The latter has never been tried, but it should. A United States of Eurasia wouldn't need to be an empire."

He went on: "Russians want a decent life, like everybody else. And anti-centralist sentiment in the provinces, especially ethnically non-Russian parts of the country, runs high. In fact, this turn of event (we call it "de-moscowsation") is pretty much inevitable when the present dictatorship collapses. It is vital though that this process doesn't go out of control. Nobody needs a repetition of the Yugoslavian crisis on a much bigger scale, and with nuclear arsenal too."

The extract we publish below from A Russian in England has been translated into English for the first time, exclusively for Index, by Chkhartishvili's translator Andrew Bromfield. The passage focuses mainly on Alexander Herzen – also a Russian exile – the "epitome of a Russian free thinker finding safe haven in England," said Chkhartishvili.

"[The book] was a genre experiment. I wanted to combine essay (my thoughts on writing) with non-fiction and fiction. This symbiosis allows me to express myself as a writer in full. The book can be used as a creative writing manual by those who intend to become writers – there are lots of writers' "lifehacks" in the essay parts, but most people read it just for fun."

Sally Gimson is acting editor at Index

Beautiful People

By Boris Akunin

THE ACTION IS set in 1857. There are four characters: three remarkable men and a remarkable woman. All Russians.

Alexander Ivanovich Herzen, a political émigré, writer and publisher, left Russia ten years ago and will never return. For the last five years he has lived in England, where he arrived from France following a series of turbulent upheavals, which need not distract us here. That French life was frantic and chaotic, dominated by the concerns of the Lesser World, a world of amatory and familial relationships, but here we see a well-ordered English life. The only thing that gives Herzen's existence meaning now is service to the Greater World, a world of ideas and the common good of society. Especially so, since, in any case, nothing remains of Alexander Ivanovich's personal life, and he is sure it will never be resumed. He regards himself as an elderly individual in whom all passion has been spent forever. After all, forty-five is a serious age.

In the Greater World things are going splendidly. Following the death of the despot Nicholas, the winds of free speech are stirring in

his distant homeland, and great reforms are under discussion. Only a few years ago, Herzen and his almanac The Pole Star were of interest only to a small band of dissidents, but now the entire readership of Russia lends an ear to the voice of liberty from London. Alexander Ivanovich's newspaper The Bell made its appearance quite recently and although it is formally banned, it is read by everyone, even government ministers and the tsar himself. Sometimes on the pages of his publication Herzen appeals directly to the absolute monarch – and Alexander III takes these appeals under advisement.

All in all, an age of euphoria. One of the portents of new times is the opening of the borders, which had been almost hermetically sealed under Nicholas' regime.

"Generally speaking, with the arrival of the new reign, everything that had been restrained by force under Nicholas I flooded abroad in an irrepressible torrent. People went to study in Germany or Switzerland, they went to Vienna, Paris and London for consultations with doctors and, last but not least, they went because now everyone was permitted to go," we read in the memoirs of Natalya Tuchkova, with whom we shall shortly become acquainted.

To use a modern expression, for Russians Alexander Ivanovich has suddenly become a star, one of the "sights" of London. After gawping at →

→ Big Ben and that miracle of technology, Crystal Palace, many visitors to the city now dream of taking a peek at Herzen too – so that they will have something to tell everyone when they get back home.

This broken-hearted man had once withdrawn into obscurity in England, where nobody knew him, in order to spend the remainder of his life in solitude. "Nowhere could I find such eremitic seclusion as in London," he wrote.

But his reclusive life is now a thing of the past, and not only because Herzen has become something of a tourist attraction. A year ago our second character, Nikolai Platonovich Ogaryov, arrived and took up residence in his home.

Ogaryov is an old friend from Herzen's childhood days. Once, in their youth, they had sworn an oath on the Sparrow Hills – "to sacrifice our lives to our chosen struggle" – and they have both fulfilled this oath, paying for their idealism in arrests, exile and banishment.

Ogaryov is forty-three. He also writes and helps his comrade publish The Bell, but he has not made a name for himself.

Despite the congruence of their political views, the two friends are not much alike. While Herzen is rational to the point of pedantry, firm of purpose, sarcastic and absolutely not inclined to rapturous exaltation – in short, adult – Ogaryov is an overgrown child. Everybody loves him, he is infinitely charming, always passionately engrossed with something, emotional, generous and carefree. He used to be very rich, but he was robbed blind and now he doesn't have a penny to his name. And like a biblical bird of the air, he takes no care to weave an enduring nest.

For Herzen, who is generous even with people he does not know, this co-inhabitant is not a burden, but a joy. They love and respect each other very much. Alexander Ivanovich is also very considerate – he makes a point of not taking any important decisions without involving his friend.

However, the greatest change in the former hermit's life has resulted from the fact that now there is a young, attractive woman living under the same roof – his friend's consort, Natalya Tuchkova. I call her a "consort" because this young, strong-willed, independent-minded lady started openly living with Ogaryov when he was still married to another woman. The loving couple have overcome a myriad of obstacles to be together and in England they have an idyllic Wordsworthian "nest like a dove's".

But at the moment described, dark clouds have already gathered over Elysium and a storm is approaching. When three people living together love each other too much, the amatory energy accumulates, and it can be discharged in an unanticipated direction. The force of attraction between Herzen and Natalya Tuchkova will soon become irresistible.

To accommodate the three of them comfortably, Herzen has rented a wonderful, detached house with a garden, close to the Thames in Putney. To go "into town" from here they have to take a train or an omnibus, which departs every ten minutes, with true British punctuality. They can also sail to the city centre and further, to Greenwich, on a river steamboat – as you still can, by the way, in our time.

Their dwelling is called Laurel House. Tuchkova writes: "With its red-painted iron roof, from the outside it resembled an English farm rather than a town house, and on the garden side it was entirely shrouded in the dense foliage of ivy that wound down over its walls from their top; extending in front of the house was a large, oval meadow, with pathways running along its edges; everywhere there were bushes of lilac, fragrant jasmine and others; and in addition, there was an entire multitude of flowers, and even a small floral conservatory". All in all, practically the abode of Bulgakov's Master and Margarita, only here Margarita has a husband.

Two hearts will burst into flames, one will be broken, a firm friendship will be subjected to severe trials – and will withstand them. Natalya Tuchkova-Ogaryova will become Tuchkova-Herzen. The drama has not yet erupted, but it should be palpable in the atmosphere of the narrative, charging it with electricity. As yet, on the surface everything is still serene, the life of the jolly little commune is idyllic.

This is how things stand, when another

Russian appears in London – for only a few days, passing through.

He is our main character, a quite astounding individual.

Pavel Alexandrovich Bakhmetiev is the scion of an ancient line that can be traced back to the Tatar prince Bakhmet, who crossed over into the service of the sovereign of Moscow in the 15th century. At first glance there is absolutely nothing remarkable in this young man's biography. At the age of twenty-nine he has no special accomplishments to his name: he has merely completed the course of study at Saratov Grammar School and studied for some time at an agricultural institute.

But Bakhmetiev's teacher at the grammar school was Chernyshevsky, who will later present him in the novel What is to be Done? under the name of Rakhmetov, and the young nobleman did not study the agricultural sciences in order to manage his estate, but with a Purpose.

We'll get to the Purpose a little later, but first a few words about Pavel Alexandrovich. He is exactly like Chernyshevsky's character. Strange, taciturn, pitilessly demanding of himself. He has tempered his body and spirit with torments of every possible kind, preparing himself to serve his homeland – by which the young idealists of that time meant the revolution. However, having roamed around Rus for a while, Bakhmetiev, unlike the future agrarian-socialist Narodniks, has realised that there is nothing in his homeland worth sleeping on nails for. There will not be any revolution. Evidently this was the point at which a different Purpose took shape.

Since there was no enthusiasm for the idea of a commune in his homeland, he could build a cell of the free world of the future far away from civilisation. After reading a few books, Pavel Alexandrovich decided that the best location for realising this aim would be the Marquesas Islands, which are beautiful, pristine and free.

He studied a bit of agricultural management, not in order to earn a diploma, but to acquire essential knowledge. When he decided that he had learned enough, he moved on to action. He converted the inheritance from his father into

cash and ascertained that in order to reach the Marquesas Islands he had to go via New Zealand. To get there, he had to sail from London, and so he set out for England.

"Yes, this gentleman was a special kind of person, a representative of a very rare breed," Chernyshevsky writes in his novel. Another astonishing deed performed by Rakhmetov's prototype is also described in the book.

"There were also rumours that a young Russian, a former landowner, presented himself to the very greatest European thinker of the 19th century, the progenitor of a new philosophy, a German, and said to him: 'I have thirty thousand thalers: I only need five thousand: I ask you to take the rest...' Naturally, the philosopher did not take the money, but the Russian supposedly left it with a banker under the other man's name anyway and wrote this to him: 'Do as you wish with the money, throw it into the water if you like, but now you cannot give it back to me, you will never find me,' – and supposedly this money is still sitting there with the banker. If this rumour is correct, there is absolutely no doubt that it was Rakhmetov who presented himself to the philosopher."

The German philosopher is a – somewhat ironical – reference to Herzen, with his German surname and foreign sententiousness.

The real idealist, not the literary one, approached Herzen with his exotic proposal, because he respected him and trusted him.

One day Alexander Ivanovich received a letter from a stranger, who requested an urgent meeting. The urgency was motivated by the fact that this individual was sailing for New Zealand in a few days, but before taking his leave of the Old World, he wished "to do something useful for Russia".

Pavel Alexandrovich Bakhmetiev brought →

→ with him 50,000 francs (not 30,000 thalers). He had calculated that such a large amount was not required for his commune, 30,000 would be enough. He asked Herzen to take the rest for "propaganda work", adding "however, make whatever use of it you wish". Pavel Alexandrovich had no doubt that Herzen would use the capital for the good of the cause.

Alexander Ivanovich behaved irreproachably. First of all, he tried to persuade the dreamer to abandon his bizarre plan. Then he agreed to accept the money, but exclusively for safekeeping, spending only the interest for a period of ten years – in case Bakhmetiev might change his mind and come back. And he set an additional condition: Ogaryov must endorse this contract and be its second guarantor.

Bakhmetiev went to Laurel House, where a further, expanded meeting took place. He didn't want to take a receipt – his friends thrust it on him almost by force.

After that Herzen took the traveller to the Rothschild Bank, deposited the 20,000 in an account at five per cent annual interest and recommended that Bakhmetiev should convert the 30,000 to gold. Pavel Alexandrovich tipped the heap of money into some kind of sheet, tied it in a knot, and sailed away to the back of beyond, from where he never returned. What happened to him, whether he succeeded in founding a commune or perished on his journey, no one knows. This mystery has intrigued many researchers since then. In the 1960s, Natan Eidelman carried out his own investigation. In particular, he established that Bakhmetiev very probably sailed on the clipper Acasta, which left London on the first of September, 1857 (this was the only ship that set out for New Zealand at that time). But it proved impossible to obtain the passenger list, and no indications of Bakhmetiev's presence in New Zealand were discovered either. Pavel Alexandrovich disappeared in a highly romantic fashion, leaving behind a beautiful memory of himself, as well as an entirely material reminder in the form of the "Bakhmetiev Fund" – the name by which the capital he left behind came to be known among Russian revolutionaries. The sum

was fairly trifling, something like $200,000 in today's terms, but for the perpetually impecunious "crusaders against the regime", this was huge money. Many of them tried to obtain it from Herzen, but Alexander Ivanovich kept his word and only paid out the interest for "propaganda".

Unfortunately, the monetary thread of this marvellous story has an ugly ending, because money in general is not very beautiful.

Ten years went by. Bakhmetiev dissolved into the vast oceanic expanses. And the revolutionary Nechaev – the same individual whom Dostoevsky portrayed in The Devils as Petrusha Verkhovensky – showed up to see Herzen and spun him a heap of hokum about being a really important member of the underground. Herzen did not believe him. Then Nechaev duped the over-credulous Ogaryov, who gave the swindler his half of the money. At this point Herzen passed away and gullible Nikolai Platonovich gave Nechaev everything that was left, although he himself was living in poverty.

After Ogaryov's beloved wife left him for his best friend he went through a period of depression, drinking constantly. He was saved from total and absolute ruination by the English prostitute Mary, who became his wife. She cared for Nikolai Ivanovich until he died. All exactly like the progressive novels of the time, in which a noble man saves a "fallen woman", only the other way round – it was the fallen Mary who saved Ogaryov.

They write that he aged early and was already a decrepit old man by the age of sixty. His health was poor and he drank every now and then, but to his very last day, he lived for ideas

and the cause of freedom. He died after missing his footing and injuring himself badly (he had always been ungainly, and on this occasion, he was probably also drunk). He died in Greenwich, in his Mary's arms: "He longed to set the whole world free, and make each person happy. Yet dangling by a thread was he, a soldier cut from paper." Okudzhava's song fits Ogaryov to a tee.

Natalya Tuchkova was the only one of our characters who returned to Russia. She outlived the men by a long time and left us her memoirs about them, for which we are very grateful.

All this is sad. Beautiful, but sad.

The Assignment

You have to write a romantic novella – this is almost the only genre, in which the wholesale likeability of the populace does not seem preposterous. Romanticism is when very beautiful people live very beautiful lives. In short – absolutely our case here. But even if you do not like Revolutionary Democrats at all, and their creed does not seem beautiful to you, love them for the present, become them – we have already said that a writer must be able to become absolutely anyone.

Write so that the reader will feel a pleasant tickling sensation in his nose, forget the mortgage for a while and think: perhaps I should just say to hell with everything and sail away to Alexandr Grin's town of Zurbagan?

Only remember that you should not overdo the sugarcoating. And for this reason, we shall not take as our literary model the jellied-fruit candy style of the leading Russian romantic, but the impish mockery of the novel What Is to Be Done? – especially since the spirit of Chernyshevsky hovers over our storyline in any case. I must say that I like this work. It was my good fortune not to read it in the ninth class of school, out of laziness. I limited myself to the textbook exegesis, and only discovered the book itself at a mature age. I fell totally in love with the novel – not for the absurdities preached in it, but for its adrenaline-driven vigour, its endearing faith that reason is bound to triumph. (In point of fact, this is by no means certain, but we shall leave that for the next lesson.)

Chernyshevsky feels uncomfortable with pretty flourishes and therefore treats them sarcastically:

"Decent people have started meeting together. And how can this possibly fail to happen more and more often, with the number of decent people increasing with every new year? With time, this will become an entirely ordinary occurrence, and with more time, there will cease to be any other occurrences, because all people will be decent people. Then everything will be very good."

Sincere love and hope can be sensed in the author's scoffing tone, and this is more beautiful than any smooth, vapid writing style.

But in our case the problem of excess sugar cannot be solved simply by lowering the style. The motive force of any plot is confrontation. Life is boring when there is no struggling. But here, as in socialist realism, you will have a very limited space for collisions: the conflict of the good with the better. As in Gogol – the sweet bickering of a "pleasant lady" with a lady who is "pleasant in every respect":

"This way, this way, into this little nook here!" said the hostess, seating her guest in the corner of the sofa. "That's it! That's it. And here's a cushion for you!"

Muddle through any way you like, but it must not be boring. And that, by the way, is an indispensable condition of the assignment set for every one of our lessons. Only serious literature can be boring, but popular fiction – never.

To Sail or Not to Sail?
A SHORT STORY

An Eccentric

On one of the final days of summer in the year 1857, a young man disembarked from the Dover train at London's Waterloo Station. It was obvious immediately that he was a foreigner, yet he himself was convinced that he looked like a genuine Briton, for he was wearing a jockey cap on his head and had a tartan rug across his shoulders. No one in London ever dressed in this freakish manner, and apart from that, it was a very hot →

→ August day. The new arrival, however, had trained himself to ignore the weather conditions. He had acquired his present outfit immediately before leaving St Petersburg, from a junk stall at the Sennoi Market, because the traveller's intentions, on arriving in England, included that of "merging entirely with the natives".

On glancing round and observing that no one in the crowd was paying the slightest attention to him (you cannot surprise Londoners with eccentrics and foreigners), the young man felt most gratified.

"Excellent!" he told himself cheerfully in Russian. "Now, where do you keep your cabbies around here?"

A row of cabs was standing on the station square.

"Far to Khotel Sablonier?" The Russian asked a driver.

He had taught himself English, learning twenty words a day, and he knew many, but he pronounced them as they were written. The cab-driver, however, understood that the foreigner was asking about the Hôtel Sablonnière on Leicester Square and quoted him a crazy price: one shilling and two pence.

This mattered not a whit to the young man, he never used cabbies on principle. What for, if you have a sound pair of legs?

"Far?" he repeated.

"Very far."

The cabman gestured broadly to the north, beyond the river Thames.

The Russian nodded, took a firmer grip on his unimpressive luggage – a carpet travelling bag and a small calico bundle – and set out in the direction indicated with a long, rapid stride.

At an earlier time, he had walked round almost half of Russia in exactly the same way, sometimes covering fifty versts a day. A mile or two was nothing to a walker like that.

But it is time for us to introduce this eccentric. In Foreign Passport No. 3338, issued by the administrative office of the Governor of Saratov Province, he was identified as Pavel Alexandrovich Bakhmetiev, a non-serving nobleman, 29 years of age. We could take a very long time telling his story, since in many respects he was a remarkable individual, but we can also be brief. It will probably suffice to explain why, out of hundreds of hotels in London, he had chosen the little-known Sablonnière. Someone had told Bakhmetiev that when Ivan Sergeyevich Turgenev was in England, he stayed at this hotel. Several years earlier, while still a grammar-school student, Pavel Bakhmetiev had read Turgenev's story "Mumu", which had shaken him to the depths of his soul, following which he had firmly and irrevocably determined to devote his life to the struggle against slavery. All of Bakhmetiev's decisions were firm and irrevocable and his mental attitude was methodical. No task was immense enough to frighten him, but he considered it necessary to ascertain whether it was physically feasible. Pavel Alexandrovich had spent several years "studying the subject" – it was with this purpose that, as we have already mentioned, he had trudged around half of his native land. As for the conclusion that he had reached – we shall get to that later.

At the Hôtel Sablonnière the young man took the cheapest room, just under the roof. The first thing he did was to send a letter by city post to an address written on a piece of paper. Then he took a look out of the window at London's liveliest square. Its gaslights glowed enticingly (evening had already set in), but Bakhmetiev was not attracted by the temptations of civilisation. He had an enquiring mind, but he was not inquisitive. As we know, the difference between these two qualities is that an inquisitive person takes an interest in everything and anything, while a person with an enquiring mind is only concerned with what they need for the task at hand.

Bakhmetiev decided the best thing would be to get a good sleep. He was able to sleep at any time of the day or night, and, if necessary, could go without any sleep at all for days on end.

He didn't like the look of the bed, especially the mattress. Any other guest would have considered it lumpy and hard, but Bakhmetiev was accustomed to sleeping in a different style. He dragged the mattress down onto the floor, together with the sheet and pillow. Then he took a strange object out of his carpet bag – a thin pallet, studded all over with drawing-pins – and stretched out imperturbably on this torturous item of bedding. Pavel Alexandrovich's skin was as tough as leather, and well used to such treatment.

A minute later the ascetic was soundly asleep.

A Moral Sybarite

Alexander Ivanovich Herzen valued a state of ease above everything else in the world; he was traumatised by any kind of suffering, or even simple discomfort. In fact, "comfort" was his favourite word. For instance, if he wished to say that a certain action was unacceptable to him, he said: "I would find that uncomfortable".

However, this individual's ideas concerning comfort were not entirely commonplace. He put up with hardships, and even dangers, rather easily (all sorts of things had happened in his uneven life), but he absolutely could not tolerate emotional unease. Herzen could be plunged into this state – which, it must be admitted, is extremely unpleasant – by something entirely extraneous, to which a normal person would not have given a second thought. Such as, for instance, news of famine in Calcutta or mass floggings of peasants in Poltava Province, although our Alexander Ivanovich had never even been in India or Little Russia. Nonetheless, he was unable to recover his state of ease and comfort until he had made a contribution to support the starving or responded to the hideous crime in the province of Poltava – he was such a great moral sybarite.

He always spent the morning reading his voluminous correspondence, the bulk of which arrived from Russia. The address written on the envelopes was often simply "Mr Herzen in London". There were so many letters that Her Majesty's Postal Service had learned to identify them and forward them directly to Putney, where the famous exile lived.

Most of the letters told of sundry atrocities in Russia, and Herzen suffered torment as a result. This, however, was useful. The powerful emotions were subsequently vented in fervent social and political essays.

Setting aside the sheets of paper on which places circled in red stood out like bleeding wounds, Herzen pulled another little pile of city post towards him. The pleasant items – a letter from Louis Blanc, an invitation to pasta from Giuseppe Mazzini, a catalogue of new acquisitions from a book shop – he set aside for the time being. He moved two envelopes closer. Their senders were denoted by two unfamiliar Russian names. As the most famous Russian in England, Alexander Ivanovich often received appeals from compatriots who were in need of help, usually financial in nature. It was uncomfortable to refuse. From long ago, he had imposed a "seventh-part" tax on himself – he reserved one seventh of his income for appeasing his moral susceptibility: helping those, whom it was impossible not to help. Dividing all incoming sums by seven was inconvenient, but Alexander Ivanovich liked figures and he had no fear of fractions. He had imposed a similar "sennight" tax on his own time: every seventh day, on Sunday, he kept an open house for émigrés. Most of them lived in straitened circumstances and they came, not only to socialise with each other, but also simply to eat their fill. The host found these gatherings wearisome, because for the most part émigrés are a tedious and peevish crowd, but after all, for many of them Herzen's Sundays were their only escape from the drab confines of life in a foreign land.

One of the Russian letters was from a student who didn't have enough money for a ticket home, to Moscow. Alexander Ivanovich put two one-pound notes into an envelope and made ➜

→ a corresponding entry in his account book. The "seventh-part" funds for this month were already exhausted, he had to add something taken from the funds allocated for his own personal pleasures. For instance, he could buy slightly cheaper tobacco, that was quite all right, or – even better – smoke two cigars instead of three, that would also be better for his health.

The second letter made its recipient sigh. A certain Bakhmetiev, who was staying at the thoroughly bourgeois Hôtel Sablonnière – that is, he was obviously a man of means – sought to lay claim to something more precious than money – Herzen's time: he requested a meeting, and an urgent one at that.

The letter could have been ignored and left unanswered, but there was a palpable nervous energy in the angular, inelegant handwriting, in the clumsiness of the style, and Alexander Ivanovich sensed genuine urgency in the phrase "you would oblige me greatly, the matter will not brook delay, for I have very little time". Perhaps this person had a fatal illness, or faced some acute emergency? Was this not the way that people about to commit suicide wrote, clutching at a straw? A normal person would have told himself: And what's that to me? But moral sybaritism is a subtle business.

"I intend to visit the printshop in any case, from there it's not far to Leicester Square," Herzen told himself. "That really would be better than this person turning up here and devouring the whole day."

And he immediately felt more comfortable.

A Strange Conversation

Mr Bakhmetiev did not resemble a suicidal individual in the least and, judging from his broad shoulders and ruddy features, his health in general was quite excellent. When asked what the reason for his request was and, most importantly, why it was so urgent, he didn't reply – that is, he literally said nothing and merely gazed at his unexpected visitor, occasionally blinking his wide-set eyes.

After waiting for a while, Alexander Ivanovich started feeling annoyed. It occurred to him that this was an ordinary "tourist", as he called his otiose compatriots, who came to take a look at the sites of the British capital, one of which the famous publisher of The Pole Star, and now The Bell, had become.

"Listen here, my dear sir, if you have nothing to say to me, why in hell's name did you write to me?" Herzen enquired sternly: he was capable of discourtesy with dunces.

"I love Russia very much. As do you," Bakhmetiev replied irrelevantly and hesitated. After that he kept hesitating all the time. He was evidently a man more accustomed to internal monologue than dialogues. "But I have made a point of walking all around it, looking at it and unriddling it. It will be a long time before living there becomes interesting for someone like me. Not in my lifetime."

"Someone like you?" asked Herzen, intrigued.

The young man gestured vaguely.

"I can't explain. Gerasims on all sides. Mu-mu, mu-mu, and the master gives the orders . . ." He lost his thread. "Anyway, being there is not to my liking. I have thought of something else."

Alexander Ivanovich no longer regretted having come. His curiosity was piqued.

"I want to build a different life. With people who are equal and free. At liberty. On an island, somewhere, far away. So that no one will hinder me."

"On what island would that be?"

"Here, look," the incomprehensible fellow replied, becoming animated. Reaching into his travelling bag, he extracted a folded map and opened it out. "In the Marquesas Islands. Do you see the little yellow dots in the Pacific Ocean? I read about them in Kruzenshtern's Voyage. A very good place, apparently. I'll set up home and pick up some comrades. And we'll start living differently from everyone else, the right way."

"A madman," thought Alexander Ivanovich, looking at the map.

"Don't think that I'm some kind of crank," Bakhmetiev declared, as if he had overheard. "I've thought everything through. I'll sail to New Zealand, stock up with everything necessary, and from there – to the island, Nuku Hiva. I have money, an inheritance from my late father."

He pointed to the bundle lying beside his travelling bag. Seeing his companion's bewildered expression, he untied the cloth. Lying inside it were bundles of paper money.

"There's fifty thousand francs here. I collected it in Paris against a letter of credit."

"You carry it around just like that, in a cloth bundle?" Herzen asked in amazement. "But then, that's your business. I simply don't see the point of expounding your... interesting plans to me."

"The point is that I don't need that much. I've calculated everything. Thirty thousand will be enough for the passage and the commune. Before I leave, I want to do something for Russia. I thought about it and decided that you know better than I do how to spend twenty thousand to good purpose. The money is superfluous to me."

Alexander Ivanovich realised immediately that this was not a joke. He could tell from Bakhmetiev's manner that he didn't know how to joke.

"Which precise purpose did you have in mind?"

"I don't know. Something that will make people want freedom. I'll count out twenty bundles right away and won't detain you any longer."

The young man apparently thought everything had been said and there was nothing more to add.

"Wait!" Herzen cried out. "Pavel... Alexandrovich..." – he couldn't immediately recall Bakhmetiev's patronymic. "This is inconceivable! I cannot accept such a substantial sum – actually, any sum – from someone I've never seen before, and with such indefinite instructions . . . Without witnesses! No, it is impossible!" Then an idea that might solve the problem occurred to him. "I'll tell you what, come to see me at home tomorrow. An old friend of mine, almost a brother, will be there, Mr Ogaryov."

"I know that name," Pavel Alexandrovich said with a nod. "He was exiled, wasn't he? That means he's a worthy individual."

"Extremely worthy. He can be the witness and the guarantor."

Bakhmetiev suddenly frowned:

"At your home? I suppose you have a wife?"

"No. I'm a widower," Alexander Ivanovich replied drily, making it clear that this was not a subject for conversation, and even condolences would be excessive.

But offering condolences didn't even occur to his odd companion.

"That's very good!" he exclaimed in relief. But the next moment he realised this sounded awkward and he became embarrassed. "I didn't mean it's a good thing that you were widowed, it's just that I always feel embarrassed in the presence of ladies."

Herzen burst out laughing – the apologetic young man really did look very comical.

"Don't count your chickens just yet. A lady will be there too, and a spirited lady at that!"

A Troubled Soul

Natalya Alexeievna took a long time summoning up her courage before going down to the drawing room on the ground floor. Just recently she had been late all the time – for meals, and for going out when the three of them were due to take a walk or a drive to visit someone. She had to prepare herself or, as she called it, "gird on her armour". But somehow it protected her less and less, that armour.

Having steeled herself and even gone out onto the stairway, she froze again halfway down.

Below her she heard a jolly voice say:

"Good gracious, why on nails?"

A different, toneless voice replied:

"I took the idea from the life of a certain ascetic monk. In his cave he slept 'on a board studded with nails in disdain of the flesh'. Who knows what hardships there might be on Nuku Hiva? Only I don't sleep on nails, but on drawing pins, you know, the kind they use for pinning up paper. I tried nails. You don't sleep very well."

"I should say not!" exclaimed a third party to the conversation, bursting into merry, childish laughter. "Ah, where's Natasha got to? She should hear this!"

The first voice was Iskander's, the second must belong to that crank, Bakhmetiev, and the third belonged to Kolya – he was Natalya Alexeievna's husband. On hearing her own name, the young woman blenched, turned back and started walking upwards again, trying not to make the steps creak.

➔

→ "You despicable, despicable wretch," she whispered in anguish.

Anguish had taken up residence in her heart two weeks earlier, on that day when the three of them went boating on the Thames and clumsy Kolya (he was rowing) swayed the boat. Natalya Alexeievna, who had just stood up in order to reach out to the picnic hamper, lost her balance and fell straight onto Iskander, and he caught her in his arms. Everything suddenly went dark, she could scarcely breathe, a hot tremor ran through her body, it went completely limp – and Natalya Alexeievna realised with horror that she loved him, she loved him beyond all endurance. That is, she had loved him before, of course – as Kolya's closest friend, as a fine person and, in general, as Herzen, but there is love, and there is Love. God only knew when the former had grown into the latter, but the trivial incident in the boat had opened Natalya Alexeievna's eyes to the nightmarish reality of her situation.

If you gathered together all the men living in the world, from Lapland to Patagonia, Iskander was the only one whom she must never, under any circumstances, admit into her heart. Poor, wonderful, vulnerable Kolya would never survive the double betrayal. And worst of all, it would be so vulgar! All those discussions and dreams about Russia, about wonderful ideas and the humankind of the future, and in the outcome – an absolutely banal case of adultery. What hideous ignominy.

It was a good thing that the men, in their convenient, perennial blindness, had not guessed about anything. Natalya Alexeievna had sworn to herself that she would scorch this shameful weakness out of her heart with red-hot iron. And if that didn't work, she could simply up and leave both of them. At least that would be honest.

Cheered by this new idea, she finally pulled herself together and ran down.

"I'm sorry," she said cheerfully on entering the drawing room, "I became engrossed in reading Flaubert. Now there's a writer who understands women!"

"A most insensitive remark in the presence of another writer," Iskander replied jokingly.

The men stood up. Bakhmetiev squeezed the lady's fingers more tightly than necessary, became embarrassed and jerked his hand away. He was plain, but likeable enough. Natalya Alexeievna deliberately did not look at the other two.

"Ah, Nathalie, what a story you missed!" her husband told her reproachfully. "Just imagine, Pavel Alexandrovich walked along the Volga with barge-haulers. And he got a job with an artel of loaders."

"What for?" she asked, touching her left cheek. It was burning, because Iskander was standing on her left, close.

"I needed to find out if Rousseau was correct about the usefulness of simple labour for developing the personality," Bakhmetiev explained. "He was not. Arduous physical labour is degrading and it reduces a human being to a beast of burden. In the future it will be carried out by machines, and then equality will be possible. But not before that."

It was a familiar kind of Russian conversation. Natalya Alexeievna started feeling calmer.

"And what have you decided to do with the twenty thousand?" she asked Iskander, even managing to look him in the eye.

"Two things. The money will be managed by Nikolai and myself. I shall place it with Rothschild for ten years, at five per cent. If Pavel Alexandrovich changes his mind, the money will be returned to him. These terms to be secured by a written undertaking."

"No written undertaking is needed," Bakhmetiev declared agitatedly. "And I don't need the ten years either. Just take it and have done with it."

"We cannot agree on any other terms," Iskander snapped. "You will have to find other beneficiaries."

"How magnificently benevolence and strength are combined in him," Natalya Alexeievna thought and turned away.

"Very well," the chump sighed. "If you insist, let there be a written undertaking."

"And there's another thing," said Iskander, after a moment's thought. "Since we shall be going to Rothschild's to formalise the matter, I would advise you to exchange your money for

gold. Owing to imminent events in Italy, the exchange rate of the paper franc is unreliable. While you are sailing to the Pacific Ocean, Little Napoleon could totally destroy his currency. It is already listed at zero point nine five."

"Are there any areas of learning that he is not well-informed about?" Natalya Alexeievna thought as she sat beside her husband. She felt very happy and very wretched.

A Barricade and a Ditch

On their way to Greenwich, they spoke first about Natalya Alexeievna. Ogaryov was concerned about his wife's health. Just recently her migraines and bouts of melancholy had been more frequent: she either became very agitated, or started weeping uncontrollably for no reason. Her mood swings were unpredictable. Take today, for instance. She herself had said: "Let's all go together to see the eccentric off on his voyage," – and at the last moment, just before we left the house, it was: "No, go without me".

"Women have all kinds of quirks. They are not like us," Iskander replied to that as he gazed at the murky water of the Thames, through which a small municipal steamboat was splashing its paddle-wheels. "Anna Alexeievna's foibles are mere trifles, brother."

And he sighed, recalling his own deceased wife.

Nikolai Platonovich flung up his arms, struck by a sudden thought.

"Listen! Maybe she could be pregnant? That would be a real turn-up! We'd given up hoping."

Alexander Ivanovich's eyebrows merged together on his high forehead.

"Very possibly," he responded somewhat dryly and changed the subject. "I was just thinking what a loss it is for Russia that people like Bakhmetiev abandon her for such far-distant lands, for a mere chimera, anything to be as far away as possible. They'll be needed when the storm breaks, won't they? Exactly their kind of people. After all, there aren't many of these Bakhmetievs in the world. But when the time of testing arrives, without champions like them the revolution will become bogged down. On his Marquesas Islands he won't even find out about it."

"Never mind, on the bright side, you and I are here. I, for instance, will go straight back to Russia just as soon as the barricades appear there!" declared Nikolai Platonovich, shaking his fist defiantly in the direction of the Greenwich Pier as it moved closer. They could already see the masts of the clipper on which Bakhmetiev would set out for New Zealand.

"I can just imagine you on a barricade," Herzen said with a smile. "With your agility, you'll tumble down off it and break your neck."

His friend shrugged light-heartedly.

"A gypsy woman foretold that I would die after tripping over my own feet. Better break my neck on a Russian barricade than an English road – and he gestured at the roofs of the quiet London suburb.

A quarter of an hour later, at the long-voyage mooring, beside the three-masted barque "Acasta", which was ready to depart, they both tried to persuade Bakhmetiev to see reason, adducing the aforementioned argument and sundry others, no less convincing.

Pavel Alexandrovich listened without interrupting. He also waited for a little while after Herzen and Ogaryov fell silent – in case they might have more to say. Then he explained:

"Things in Russia will not become interesting soon, and I can't wait. I'm no longer young, I'm already thirty. I want to devote my life to action, not conversation."

And that was all he said.

As previously, he was holding only a travelling bag and small bundle, but now it was a heavy one.

"What have you got there, gold coins?"   →

→ Herzen asked incredulously. "The entire one and a half thousand napoleons?"

Bakhmetiev nodded.

"They don't fit into the carpet bag."

"For God's sake, they jangle! You'll be robbed and killed! You should have bought a bag with a lock!"

"I don't want to spend the money. It belongs to the future commune. And robbing me isn't easy – I'm strong," Pavel Alexandrovich replied.

A bell sounded on deck. The small number of passengers started saying goodbye to the people seeing them off.

"Will we meet again?" asked Herzen, agitated for some reason. "If things don't work out there, come back. Your money's waiting for you. And write from Wellington."

"I don't know how to come back to a place. And I'm not in the habit of writing either."

"Well, in that case, I'll write, for collection. If there's some kind of post office there."

"It won't reach me. I've changed my name. England isn't Russia. Here they take what you say on trust and don't ask for a document. I simply called myself by a different name, and they wrote it down. Goodbye, gentlemen. You are probably the last Russians I'll see."

He shook both of them by the hand, for which he had to set the jangling bundle down on the wooden planking, and then walked up the gangway, without glancing back.

Even afterwards, when the ship cast off and started moving away, he didn't come out to wave.

Watching as the "Acasta" departed, pulled in the direction of the sea by a panting tugboat, Ogaryov asked:

"Tell me, do you sometimes also feel like sailing off to somewhere far, far away, to a different life from which you can never return, and there is no reason to return anyway?"

Alexander Ivanovich chuckled.

"'To sail or not to sail? That is the question. Whether 'tis nobler in the mind to suffer the slings and arrows of outrageous fortune, or to take arms against a sea of troubles, and by opposing end them?' Is that what you're asking about? Of course I do. Everyone sometimes wants to sail

off into a different life and never look back. But the thing is, that someday, whether you want to or not, you will sail away in any case, there's no escaping it. So why be in such a great hurry?"

Commentary

One possible way out of a difficult storyline situation – the absence of confrontation that I warned you about in the Assignment – is to switch the narrative motor's fuel from events to atmosphere.

Nothing special happens, all the interest is focused on the characters. Each one of them, even the scarcely adumbrated Ogaryov, adds his own element of coloration to this impressionistic canvas.

The other device used here is what I call "the haiku effect". It is only possible when you are sure that the reader possesses certain supplemental knowledge. You press hidden levers that prompt the reader to make a certain mental effort and experience the feelings you require. The most elementary example is my favourite tercet by the poetess O-Chiyo (I once composed a very hefty novel around it – The Diamond Chariot):

Dragonfly-catcher,
Oh, how very far away
You have run today!

(In order to appreciate the meaning, you need to know that the haiku was written on the death of a three-year-old son.)

It is the same here. I have exploited the fact that the reader already knows from the preparatory materials:

- that Natalya Alexeievna will not scorch out her love with red-hot iron;
- that poor Ogaryov will break his neck in that very same Greenwich at which he gestured so dismissively;
- that Bakhmetiev will disappear without trace. ✖

Translated by **Andrew Bromfield**

53(03):86/98|DOI:10.1177/03064220241285716

Song for Stardust

In 1985 Ireland's greatest folk musician **CHRISTY MOORE** wrote a song about a nightclub fire where 48 died. It was banned but this year he was finally vindicated, writes **JESSICA NÍ MHAINÍN**

FOLK MUSICIAN CHRISTY Moore has always had his finger on the pulse of Irish society, with many of his songs taking in political and social commentary. More than 40 years ago, one of his songs was banned. He was only fully vindicated this year.

In July 1985, just days after his album Ordinary Man was released, Moore's record label received a legal letter. The subject of the letter was the song They Never Came Home, which was about a fire that killed 48 young people and injured over 200 in the Dublin Stardust nightclub on Valentine's Day in 1981. Most of those who died were from working class areas of the city.

Through their solicitors, the wealthy Butterly family (who owned the nightclub) claimed that They Never Came Home was in contempt of court and would prejudice the outcome of litigation concerning over 200 compensation claims arising from the fire.

Although 12,000 copies of the album

ABOVE: Folk singer Christy Moore faced legal action over a song telling the story of an Irish tragedy

had been distributed and it was already at number one in the charts, Moore's record label immediately went about recalling it and contacting radio stations to urge them not to play the song in case the allegation was upheld. Moore, his producer and his record label all stood to be impacted by the application to the court from Eamon Butterly, ➔

Hundreds of Boys and Girls injured and maimed / All because the fire exits were chained

→ Scott's Foods Ltd and Silver Swan Ltd (companies owned by the family, which were linked with Stardust).

The contempt case was seen urgently by the High Court on 9 August 1985. Among the arguments put forward by the Butterly family was that it was inaccurate to state, as the song did, that "the fire exits were chained". They also said it was inaccurate to state that "no one" could tell how the fire started, because a previous investigation had found the likely cause to have

been arson. That finding was strongly disputed by the families at the time and for many years afterwards.

An affidavit from Moore was read to the court stating that the subject of the song was, in his opinion, a matter of public and social concern. Many of those affected by the fire came out to support him.

Nonetheless, the judge found that the song was in contempt of court. Costs were awarded against Moore and, in total, the legal action ended up

costing him and his team the equivalent of 100,000 Irish punt, estimated to be around €300,000 ($335,000) in today's money. The song could no longer be promoted, distributed or sold in shops in Ireland. They Never Came Home had effectively been banned.

After a long campaign by the families, an inquest into the Stardust tragedy was finally opened in April 2023. After hearing testimony from over 370 witnesses, including former nightclub staff, emergency responders, survivors and fire experts, the jury returned their verdict earlier this year.

Not only were the fire exits found to have been chained shut, but the fire was deemed to have been started by an electrical fault, likely owing to the system having been overloaded. The

They Never Came Home

By CHRISTY MOORE

St Valentine's Day comes around once a year,
All our thoughts turn to love as the time it draws near,
Sweethearts and darlings, husbands and wives,
Pledge love and devotion for the rest of their lives.
As day turns to evening soon night-time does fall,
Young people prepare for the Valentine's Ball,
As the night rings with laughter some families mourn
The 48 children who never came home.

Down to the Stardust they made their way
The bouncers stood back as they lined up to pay
Records are spinning there was dancing as well
Just how the fire started no one can tell.
In a matter of seconds confusion did reign
The room was in darkness fire exits were chained
The firefighters wept, they could not hide,
Their sorrow and anger for those still inside.

Have we forgotten the suffering and pain
the survivors and victims of the fire in Artane,

the mothers and fathers forever to mourn
the 48 children who never came home.

All around the city the bad news it spread
There's a fire in the Stardust there's 48 dead
Hundreds of Boys and Girls injured and maimed
All because the fire exits were chained.
Our leaders were shocked, grim statements were made
They shed tears in the graveyard as the coffins were laid
The injured were abandoned year after year
Seems like our leaders shed crocodile tears.

Millions paid out on legal fees,
A fortune paid over to Butterly
In Poppintree, Coolock, Bonnybrook and Artane
Families abandoned time and again
Days turn to weeks, weeks turn to years
Our laws favour the rich or so it appears
A woman still waits for her kids to come home
Injustice breeds anger and that's what's been done.

Have we forgotten the suffering and pain
the survivors and victims of the fire in Artane,
the mothers and fathers forever to mourn
the 48 children who never came home.

Stardust fire is often described as the greatest tragedy in the history of the Irish State.

As he approaches his 80th birthday and continues to captivate audiences with his energy and emotive music, Moore gave an exclusive interview to Index, explaining what prompted him to write the song, what he remembers about the legal challenge and what he seeks to change using his music.

INDEX You have said that you write songs about things that affect you, and you are widely known for your social commentary. Where does that comes from?

CHRISTY MOORE I became aware of social injustice at an early age. Both our parents were active in local politics. A lot of my repertoire comes from other writers. My own songs come from what I see and hear around me. I began singing songs of The Clancy Brothers, then I began to look into old books of song collections. In my 20s I heard the songs of Woody Guthrie and Ewan MacColl, which opened me up to the possibility of writing new songs myself... 60 years on I'm still gathering, writing, singing.

INDEX In 1981 the Stardust fire happened. I understand the idea for the song came to you the day after the tragedy, when you heard a mother speaking about her children who had died. Did you foresee what the song would come to mean to the victims and their families? Did you personally know of anyone who was affected?

CHRISTY MOORE Over the past 40 years I have befriended many family members

from the Stardust collective. I did not know any of the Stardust victims or their families prior to 14 February 1981. I had no notion how the song might be perceived. [The fact] that the families embraced the song so wholeheartedly meant a lot to me.

INDEX What do you remember about that day you got the legal letter? Had you imagined that you could have faced legal action as a result of the song?

CHRISTY MOORE Two outstanding memories of the day: Judge Murphy displayed distaste towards me and to my work... he quoted lyrics from other songs in his summary. My strongest memory is the support I received [from] a large number of Stardust victims who attended the court case to support me.

INDEX One of the lines that was subject to the legal challenge was "hundreds of children are injured and maimed and all just because the fire exits were chained" — and earlier this year, the inquest returned a verdict showing that line to have been completely accurate. How did you feel when you heard that verdict?

CHRISTY MOORE I was overjoyed for the families when I heard the verdict. For 43 years they have struggled to gain justice for the 48. Along the way they were knocked back by two judges, numerous Taoisigh, ministers and deputies who looked the other way but they never gave up....

INDEX The other line in the song that was subject to the legal challenge was "just how the fire started, sure no one can tell". It seemed to question, or even go against, what the authorities were

saying at the time, which is that the fire had been started maliciously. Why did you decide to put in that line? Did you have a sense that the authorities were wrong?

CHRISTY MOORE It's been over 40 years since I wrote the song. I've sung it around the world more than a thousand times. Songs shift and vary across time. All I recall from the writing is a sense of anger and frustration that prevailed... I remember being in Kerry when I felt the lyric was complete. I recorded it in Artane [the Dublin suburb where the nightclub had been].

INDEX "Our laws favoured the rich - or so it appears," goes one of the lyrics in the song. Did the success of the subsequent legal action further convince you of that fact?

CHRISTY MOORE Our laws still favour the rich. I don't really see [the legal action] as a "success" but more of an admission of guilt from those who control the "system".

INDEX Human rights seems to be a theme throughout your music, given that so many of your songs advocate for those who have been mistreated or forgotten. What do you set out to change with your music?

CHRISTY MOORE Dick Gaughan, the Scottish singer, claims that all of his songs are love songs. I feel the same way about my own songs... I don't set out to change anything apart from myself. ✖

To find out more about Index's work to counter strategic lawsuits against public participation (SLAPPs), which silence public interest speech, visit the UK Anti-SLAPP Coalition's website at antislapp.uk

Jessica Ní Mhainín is head of policy and campaigns at Index

53(03):99/101|DOI:10.1177/03064220241285718

Judge Murphy displayed distaste towards me and to my work... he quoted lyrics from other songs in his summary

Put down that book!

KATIE DANCEY-DOWNS talks to **ALLISON BRACKEEN BROWN** and **AIXA AVILA-MENDOZA**, two teachers and poets whose are experts on banned books

A S ENGLISH TEACHER Allison Brackeen Brown goes about her daily life in Midland, Texas, it wouldn't be unusual for her to pass near an oil field. The area is the oil and gas capital of West Texas, and as families from Venezuela, Nigeria and elsewhere arrive to work for energy companies, they send their kids to local schools. Which is why she's had friendly warnings from colleagues about using environmental writing in her classroom.

"Just be careful, this kid's parents really took offence to this. So just know that you may have to deal with that if you choose to go down this path," she was told, and knows some colleagues have chosen to avoid using environmentally-themed articles in the classroom for this reason.

It's no secret that the more commonly censored books in US schools are those with LGBTQ+ or racial themes, but local-level censorship that's happening behind closed doors never becomes part of the official picture. Banned

Books Week 2024, starting on 22 September, comes after the American Library Association reported the highest number of challenged book titles ever documented in 2023.

And experiences like Brackeen

Friends in the Pages: A Golden Shovel Poem

By **ALLISON BRACKEEN BROWN**

You don't want me to read it because of **that?**
I've heard that at school, and have seen it on my phone. I think about it too. Is that part of me scary to **you?**
You are missing out on the other insights the story has to **give.**
Did you miss the part of the story with **them?**
There is a beauty in this friendship. It is like my own. This person who shares my story. With them I have **a**
partner to navigate this life. A person that shares my dreams and hopes. A safe place, a **home.**
A true friend accepts you for who you are. They stick with you as you change. They answer your phone call. It
   doesn't matter **when.**
Lifelong friendships don't have to make sense. Those friends, **they**
are just there. But… not all friendships last. Some friends **don't**
stick. Sometimes things fade or get too tough. Some "friends" just leave no matter what you **want.**
Friendships can be hard. Girls can be catty, with guys lines can blur. It is hard **to**
know, hard to trust, hard to believe that with you it's okay for me to just **be.**
When real life is hard there is a safe space I find **in**
books. I connect with characters whose lives look like mine, whose questions are mine. I see how friendships
   should and shouldn't be. I read **their**
stories and learn lessons, make connections. I feel less alone. Don't take these books from me.
   I don't want to do this on my **own.**

Brown's, which fall into the realms of self-censorship, are not included.

Brackeen Brown and Spanish teacher Aixa Avila-Mendoza, from Venezuela, are part of a cohort of female doctoral students based in Texas, studying the teaching of banned books. Together, they created a collection of poetry inspired by censored works, responding to each other's pieces along the way. We're publishing two of those poems here.

Brackeen Brown's golden shovel poem takes inspiration from Elizabeth Acevedo's award-winning young adult novel The Poet X, which has been challenged in various US states because the protagonist questions her Catholic faith. Its themes of race and sexuality have also been challenged. The last word of each line comes from a sentence in the book. Avila-Mendoza's blackout poem takes a page from George M Johnson's All Boys Aren't Blue, to create a new message about identity.

Avila-Mendoza works in an international school which, "especially, are bubbles," she told Index. "I am pretty sure that what you teach, even though it's an international curriculum, I'm sure there are agreements to what you can do in that country."

There might be eyes on these schools from overseas governments, and there are of course financial considerations. Avila-Mendoza taught in Qatar, and remembers self-censoring which books she taught, with other teachers saying: "Don't go there, find something else," over particular titles. She actively chose not to include the children's book Los Futbolisimos by Roberto Santiago, because it includes a kiss.

"These are things that make you think of consequences and how that can affect your whole career, just by reading a book that is good in one setting but not in another," she said.

Avila-Mendoza also taught in China, where she said that the reason she didn't experience book banning might be because the school provided a curated selection of books from which to choose.

State Your Name: A Blackout Poem

By AIXA AVILA-MENDOZA

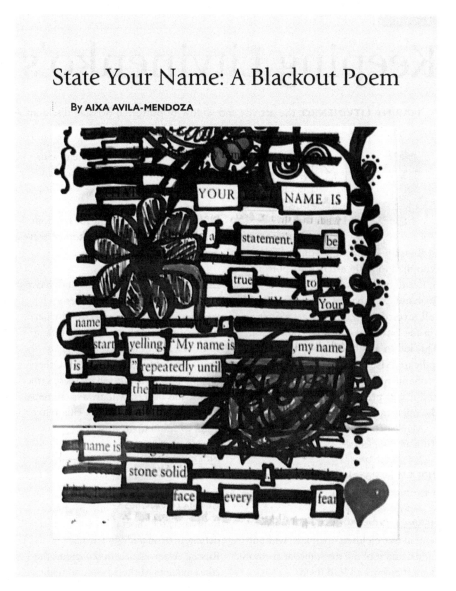

"Even if I wanted to bring a book, it had to go through customs and that's where they decide if they're going to release books or not," she said.

Meanwhile, back in Texas, the state most prone to book challenges in the USA, Brackeen Brown said there is a lot of talk at public school board meetings around banned books, with teachers self-censoring and wanting to avoid certain works for fear of the possible disapproval in their communities.

With book challenges rising and an election on the horizon, there's a big question mark over the future of the

freedom to read in the country.

"There's a part of me that wants to be idealistic, and there's a part of me that wants to be pragmatic, and there's part of me that is panicking," Brackeen Brown said. "I guess I will stick with the hopeful part of me that just feels like good literature is always going to find a way, and that good literature is always a little bit subversive." ✖

Katie Dancey-Downs is assistant editor at Index

53(03):102/103|DOI:10.1177/03064220241285734

`LAST WORD`

Keeping Litvinenko's voice alive

MARINA LITVINENKO, the activist and widow of poisoned Russian dissident Alexander Litvinenko, has the last word

MARINA LITVINENKO IS the widow of Alexander Litvinenko, a prominent opponent of Russian President Vladimir Putin, who died in 2006 after being poisoned in London. After the death of her husband, Marina led a campaign for a full investigation into the assassination via the Litvinenko Justice Foundation. This led to a public inquiry that indicated there was a strong probability the FSB was responsible and it was probable Putin was aware of the operation.

Marina continues to campaign for Russian dissidents.

INDEX Why does Russia love a strongman?

MARINA LITVINENKO Because Russians remain like children - helpless, without rights, and looking for someone to show them the way and lead them.

INDEX What do you say to those who want to cancel Russian art/literature/ music?

MARINA LITVINENKO Russia is not Putin - he is, in the end, only a man who will one day be gone; but the culture, literature and music are separate to that and will remain forever. It is also notable that some of Russia's best works of art and literature were born due to displeasure and disagreement with the country's status quo, rather than agreeing with it.

INDEX How does the fight for freedom, begun by your husband and other brave opponents of Putin, continue?

MARINA LITVINENKO My husband, having started as a professional soldier and later security officer, understood what it meant to hold that position: to fight terrorists and criminals. Putin is an amalgamation of both of these. Others like my husband, who share these same values and beliefs, will always continue to fight as long as there is a villain like Putin to stand up against.

INDEX What do you think the future holds for Russia now?

MARINA LITVINENKO While it is hard to predict, the short term will almost definitely be incredibly hard for Russia. A new generation without the consequences of the Soviet era might be able to change the country's course, and I pray that they will.

INDEX If you could save one book from the censor what would it be?

MARINA LITVINENKO My husband's book, 'Blowing up Russia'; which was banned in Russia as soon as it was published.

INDEX What work of art/culture has affected you the most?

ABOVE: The grave of Alexander Litvinenko in Highgate Cemetery in London.

MARINA LITVINENKO My first time in Rome - I could never have imagined how much of an impact the city was going to have on me; the architecture and history are unique and how it has been preserved until our time.

INDEX What future news headline would you most like to read?

MARINA LITVINENKO War in Ukraine is over. ✖

53(03):104/104|DOI :10.1177/03064220241285735

> Others will always continue to fight as long as there is a villain like Putin

CREDIT: (grave) No Swan So Fine/CC BY-SA 4.0; (portrait) Independent / Alamy